Being at Large

Being at Large

FREEDOM IN THE AGE OF ALTERNATIVE FACTS

Santiago Zabala

McGill-Queen's University Press
Montreal & Kingston • London • Chicago

© McGill-Queen's University Press 2020

ISBN 978-0-2280-0191-1 (cloth)
ISBN 978-0-2280-0192-8 (paper)
ISBN 978-0-2280-0325-0 (ePDF)
ISBN 978-0-2280-0326-7 (ePUB)

Legal deposit second quarter 2020
Bibliothèque nationale du Québec

Printed in Canada on acid-free paper that is 100% ancient forest free (100% post-consumer recycled), processed chlorine free

Funded by the Government of Canada / Financé par le gouvernement du Canada  Canada Council for the Arts / Conseil des arts du Canada

We acknowledge the support of the Canada Council for the Arts.
Nous remercions le Conseil des arts du Canada de son soutien.

Library and Archives Canada Cataloguing in Publication

Title: Being at large : freedom in the age of alternative facts / Santiago Zabala.
Names: Zabala, Santiago, 1975– author.
Description: Includes bibliographical references and index.
Identifiers: Canadiana (print) 20190235 73X | Canadiana (ebook) 20190235772 | ISBN 9780228001928 (paper) | ISBN 9780228001911 (cloth) | ISBN 9780228003250 (ePDF) | ISBN 9780228003267 (ePUB)
Subjects: LCSH: Hermeneutics.
Classification: LCC BD241 .Z33 2020 | DDC 121/.686—dc23

This book was typeset in 11/14 Sabon.

Contents

Preface vii
Introduction 3

PART ONE | BEING 13

Being and Metaphysics 20
Being and Conversation 33
Being and Truth 47

PART TWO | INTERPRETATION 59

Interpretation and Resistance 68
Interpretation and Transgression 81
Interpretation and Alteration 97

PART THREE | EMERGENCY 111

Emergency and Populism 139
Emergency and Biodiversity 145
Emergency and Revelations 150

Afterword 155
Notes 161
Index 185

Preface

An invitation from Renmin University in Beijing to deliver "Perspectives: Lectures in the Humanities" in 2017 is at the origin of this book. In these lectures I found an opportunity to divide my text around three concepts – Being, interpretation, and emergency – which have become not only near synonyms for me but also necessities for freedom in this age of alternative facts. The decision to publish this book was driven by three factors related to my previous books: the need to further clarify my ontology of remnants in relation to metaphysics, conversation, and truth; my desire to outline the anarchic vein that runs through philosophical hermeneutics, which is too often presented as a conservative discipline; and the hope to show how these two features are related to the absence of emergency now that it has become the greatest emergency in politics, the environment, and society. While readers will judge whether I achieved these goals, I hope the book will provide some insights into the meaning of freedom considering how framed our existence has become.

Earlier versions of some chapters first appeared in the following places, and I am grateful to the editors and publishers for permission to reprint: portions of part 1 were originally published as "Being and Metaphysics," in *The Routledge Companion to Hermeneutics*, edited by Jeff Malpas and Hans-Helmuth Gander (London: Routledge, 2014), 267–77; "Being Is Conversation: Remains, Weak Thought, and Hermeneutics," in *Consequences of Hermeneutics: Fifty Years after Gadamer's Truth and Method*, edited by Jeff Malpas and Santiago Zabala (Evanston, IL: Northwestern University Press, 2010), 161–76; and "Truth Absence: The Hermeneutic Resistance to Phenomenology," in *Phenomenological Variations on Truths: The Hermeneutic Challenge*, edited by Kevin Hermberg and Pol Vandevelde (New York: Continuum, 2011), 201–8. Porftions of part 2 were originally published as "The Anarchy of Hermeneutics: Interpretation as a Vital Practice," in *Inheriting Gadamer: New Directions in Philosophical Hermeneutics*, edited by Georgia Warnke (Edinburgh: Edinburgh University Press, 2016), 67–77. The introduction to part 3 includes parts from the introduction to "The Emergency of Philosophy," edited by Santiago Zabala, special issue of *Philosophy Today: An International Journal of Contemporary Philosophy* 59, no. 4 (Fall 2015): 579–82.

Among the many professors at Renmin University who attended the lectures and took part in the discussions with students I must thank in particular Yang Huilin, Xia Kejun, Zhang Xu, Wang Hai, and Zhao Jing. Once again, I'm particularly grateful to Lluís Amiguet, Arne De Boever, Arianna Letizia, Adrian Parr, Richard Polt, and Martin Woessner who improved this book in different ways. I must also thank Philip Cercone and Khadija Coxon at McGill-Queen's University Press for their constant interest in my work and providing all the help I needed. I must thank also Filippo Minelli for granting the use of one of his works of art for the cover image, which renders the idea of *Being at Large* probably better than this book does.

This book is for my friends Kate Bell and Michael Haskell.

Being at Large

Introduction

The reactions of the media prove that the situation is no better, alas, among those who boast of having remained "rational thinkers," who are indignant about the indifference to facts of the "Tweeter-in-Chief," or who rail about the stupidity of the ignorant masses. These "rational" folk continue to believe that facts stand up all by themselves, without a shared world, without institutions, without a public life, and that it would suffice to put the ignorant folk back in an old-style classroom with a blackboard and in-class exercises, for reason to triumph at last.

– Bruno Latour, *Down to Earth*

Along with Filippo Minelli's cover image, the TV series *Mr Robot* is a good example to keep in mind while reading each chapter of this book – on Being, interpretation, and emergency – as they embrace what it means to be at large, that is, free, in this age of alternative facts. The main character of the TV series, Elliot Alderson, is a cybersecurity engineer and hacker who attempts, among other things, to bring down a megacorporation that frames our freedom. The different settings that surround Minelli's photographic smoke bombs – garages, parking lots, forests – like Elliot's semi-clandestine life working for a computer security firm that helps corporations protect themselves from hackers like him, are attempts to disengage from something we've become framed within. In a world that has been framed technologically, culturally, and politically, the anarchic vein of these works reveals an emergency. But in order for this emergency to emerge it is necessary to take a hermeneutic stance against the global framed order's demand that we submit to facts, data, and reality. *Silent/Shapes* and *Mr Robot* provide paradigmatic visual and practical examples of how this can take place in the age of alternative facts.¹

The phrase "alternative facts" became popular after Kellyanne Conway, counsellor to US president Donald Trump, defended a false statement about the attendance numbers at Trump's inauguration in 2017. The problem with her phrase, which she later defined as "additional facts and alternative information," is not whether it was inaccurate or inappropriate for someone in her position to use but rather that it is a symptom of the return to order her president embodies. This return is not only political, embodied by the various right-wing populist politicians now in office throughout the world, but also cultural, an enforced move away from open societies. An open society, as Karl Popper explained while he was exiled in New Zealand and Europe was falling to authoritarian regimes, is one "in which individuals are confronted with personal decisions" as opposed to a "magical or tribal or collectivist society." In the former, no one is in possession of the ultimate truth because it is acknowledged that people have different views, interests, and values. In the latter, truth is imposed by the bearers of power. Conway's "alternative facts" is a move in the ongoing return to order, a demonstration of the imposition of truth through power.

Throughout the twentieth century other thinkers developed Popper's intuition to stress a common opposition to the universalistic aspirations of modernity: that fundamental political, moral, and cultural concepts function to denigrate and marginalize those who do not measure up to their criteria of rationality. This aspirational rationality is responsible for twentieth-century totalitarianism and colonialism and genocides, which were presented as the ultimate rational answers to questions framed by the authorities who perpetrated them. As Zygmunt Bauman explains, when "the modernist dream is embraced by an absolute power able to monopolize modern vehicles of rational action, and when that power attains freedom from effective social control, genocide follows."² Against this rational program such postmodern thinkers as Francoise Lyotard, Jean Baudrillard, and many others called for cherishing religious, social, and sexual differences rather than rejecting them in favour of a predetermined, ordered sameness.

Philosophy, Richard Rorty said, "occupies an important place in culture only when things seem to be falling apart – when cherished beliefs are threatened."³ Now that things once again are falling apart, it is crucial to recall that the so-called chaos brought about by the voiding of metanarratives through postmodernity did not aim to create a new order but to avoid the external imposition of order. This is why among the most important things postmodernity taught us is that seemingly fundamental values are not the result of a historical development toward truth but rather an agreement among social communities. As Gianni Vattimo explains, "we don't reach agreement when we have discovered the truth, we say we have discovered the truth when we reach agreement."⁴ In postmodernity these agreements are sustained by metanarratives without centre, unity, and, most of all, completion.

Since the terrorist attacks of 9/11, military occupations, neoliberal finance, and technological control have intensified drastically, to the point of creating a condition where the greatest emergency is the "absence of emergency." At the centre of these intensifications is the belief that there are no alternatives to the global framed order. We have become so alarmed (by terrorism, refugees, and financial crises) that we prefer to avoid mingling with other cultures. Nationalist right-wing populist governments are using these fears to suspend constitutional rights and enact unpopular policies. The intensification of security measures in airports, at borders, and in metropolitan areas is not justified by actual threat, as we are meant to believe, but rather are useful to erect frames around our liberties and the projects of an open society. This is why Trump's wall on the Mexican border, ban on Muslims, and hostility toward the facts of climate change are not meant to create a "state of emergency" but a condition without emergencies – where nothing can emerge from the overwhelming order. Difference, change, and cultural others must be avoided as disruptions of the safety that order is supposed to represent. This order reveals itself everyday as more authoritarian because it holds itself to be in possession of the essence of reality, defining truth for all human beings.

This return of realism is evinced by the public careers of some contemporary intellectuals, such as the psychologist Jordan Peterson, the neuroscientist Sam Harris, and philosophers like Christina Hoff Sommers and Graham Harman, among others. Although some of these thinkers would object to being categorized as new realist or politically conservative, they all seem to oppose postmodernism's neo-Marxist linguistic turn and its conflict of interpretations which holds that everything that exists is only the correlate of a subject that conceives it. The problem with this postmodern stance, they claim, is that it has denied thought any rational access to things in themselves, allowing apparently unfounded discourses on scientific objectivity, gender studies, and political values. These unfounded discourses are also responsible for an epidemic of "political correctness," which must be reversed.

This seems to be the goal of the so-called intellectual dark web, which, according to the *New York Times* writer Bari Weiss, is a movement determined to emphasize the "biological differences between men and women" and to demonstrate that "identity politics" is a threat to our social fabric.[5] The goal of these intellectuals is to present themselves as defenders of "reason," "truth," and "facts," all rational principles they claim have been corrupted by politically correct postmodernism. This is why Sommers, for example, opposes those feminists who still "believe that our society is best described as a patriarchy, a 'male hegemony,' a 'sex/gender system,'" with "factual feminism" that grounds the basic tenets of feminism in a data-driven approach.[6] These data, according to the American scholar, indicate that most feminists exaggerate the plight of women while ignoring that of men. But the ideas these authors claim to defend from politically correct opponents of truth, as Jacob Hamburger points out, are a longstanding part of the conservative tradition in the United States:

> A common refrain on the dark web is to debunk various left-of-centre critiques by arguing that what appears to

be systemic inequality is actually the result of individual choices or behavior. Hoff Sommers argues, for example, that the gender wage gap is a result of women's choices to work jobs that pay less, while Ben Shapiro believes the problem of police brutality could be solved by people – presumably African Americans – simply "avoiding interactions with the cops." On many occasions, these sorts of arguments involve uses of social science statistics that political correctness is said to ignore; on other occasions the statistics are omitted and the left's blindness to "reality" and "facts" is simply asserted or implied. In either case, the dark web's impulse when confronted with claims of inequality is almost always to deny or justify it. Either the left is making up injustices where they do not exist, the argument goes, or they disregard evidence that social disparities are in fact grounded in scientific reality.[7]

While these realist intellectuals will tell you they do not necessarily want their takes on psychology, neuroscience, or philosophy to prevail over others, in fact they are seeking to preserve a society where they find themselves at ease – that is, in which they have become more or less conscious servants of the ongoing return to order. As we can see, realism is an aspect and a consequence of dominion, not its cause. This becomes particularly evident among realist philosophers. These thinkers, under the label of "new realism," "speculative realism," or "object-oriented-ontology," aim to respond to the apparent inadequacies of postmodernity's most radical philosophies: phenomenology, hermeneutics, and deconstruction. Against Edmund Husserl, Hans-Georg Gadamer, and Jacques Derrida, the new realists return to "the secure path of science," that is, to John Searle's plan to submit philosophy to scientific methods. "The task of the philosopher," Searle declared, "is to get the problem into a precise enough form, to state the problem carefully enough, so that it admits a scientific resolution."[8] But by submitting thought to the secure path of science (or to truth in general), contemporary philosophers have fallen back into realism, the simple analysis and conservation of facts in order to help scientific disciplines take over, which was the main project of the Enlightenment. The so-called return to order or reality they promote is an attempt to more efficiently manage a system that has already collapsed.

Harman, Quentin Meillassoux, and Markus Gabriel, among others, are at the front line of this movement. Similar to Peterson and Sommers, they claim that we can have access to truth, as well as factual primary qualities of the world, without being dependent upon language or interpretation. This is why they demand a return to "a reality never exhausted by any relation to it by humans or other entities. The basic dualism in the world lies not between spirit and nature, or phenomenon and noumenon, but between things in their intimate reality and things as confronted by other things."[9] Although these thinkers have different agendas, the general idea is to return to an absolute that they understand as physical reality, a "reality" independent of us. "Contemporary philosophers," Meillassoux explains, "have lost the *great outdoors*, the *absolute* outside of pre-critical thinkers: that outside which was not relative to us, and which was given as indifferent to its own givenness to be what it is, existing in itself regardless of whether we are thinking of it or not; that outside which thought could explore with the legitimate feeling of being on foreign territory – of being entirely elsewhere."[10]

Against this return to reality, Simon Critchley and Slavoj Žižek share similar objections. Critchley considers it strange that just "when a certain strand of Anglo-American philosophy (think of John McDowell or Robert Brandom) is making domestic the insights of Kant, Hegel and Heidegger and even allowing philosophers to flirt with forms of idealism, the latest development in Continental philosophy is seeking to return to a Cartesian realism that was believed to be dead and buried."[11] And Žižek declares:

> However, in contrast to Meillassoux, I thoroughly reject the standard "realist" approach which tries to somehow distinguish in objects the way they merely appear to us and the way they are in themselves, independently of how they relate to us ... This approach of trying to subtract from the object its appearance (what we, perceiving subjects, allegedly, added to

it, the subjective excess) in order to arrive at or, rather, distil the object's In-itself, is to be rejected thoroughly. My point is that one should proceed in exactly the opposite way: subject is inscribed into the real, it touches the real, precisely at the point of the utmost "subjective" excess, in what it adds to the object, in the way it distorts the object.¹²

The aim of Critchley, Žižek, and other critics is not only to remind us how this realist philosophical approach has been surpassed already but also to show that the need for realism appears to be, as Vattimo said, a "closure that reassures and stifles at the same time." This is why the Italian philosopher believes its roots can be found "in a psychological discomfort rather than in a strictly conscious demand." The "need for reality is neurotic … because it refuses to take notice of the 'logical' need … to recognize itself as gathered within that game of interpretation that claims to be the only 'reality.'" In sum, the "need for realism is, ultimately, an effect of resentment, of the 'tedious qualities of old dogs and men who have long been kept on the leash.'"¹³ This resentment is manifest among the new realist philosophers, the "intellectual dark web" community, and right-wing populists who ask us to accept and behave in accordance with the world as it is in itself. The problem with this stance is that whoever does not submit to the ongoing reality or the absence of emergency they promote is incorrect, on the wrong side of reality, and perhaps even on the wrong side of the border. Although this return to reality is useful when it comes to telling us whether it's sunny or cloudy, can it also guide our individual existence in the age of alternative facts?

In order to understand Conway's alternative facts, as well as "post-truth" and "fake news," it is important to remember these notions are the result of the return to order and realism mention above. When she declares there is a distinction between "facts" and "additional facts or alternative information," she signals that we are entering not *the* age of alternative facts but rather *another* age of alternative facts. These successive ages of alternative arise from our naïve enthusiasm for objectivity, transparency, and free speech. This naïveté today belongs to the "rational" people Bruno Latour refers to in the epigraph. These are not only such politicians as Hillary Clinton and Emanuel Macron, who still believe that Enlightenment reasoning is an accurate model for how most people judge, but also technophiles such as Mark Zuckerberg and Evgeny Morozov, who believe conflicts can be reduced simply by improving communication among humans beings. With the advent of this age of alternative facts, all have been proven wrong.

But as philosophers of science and linguists explain, there is no "neutral observation language" that can erase human differences. These differences are not the source of our problems but rather the only possible route to their provisional solution. Facts, information, and data by themselves do nothing. "Facts remain robust," as Latour says, "only when they are supported by a common culture, by institutions that can be trusted, by a more or less decent public life, by more or less reliable media."[14] The rise of alternative facts is another indication that whether a statement is believed depends less on its reality than on the conditions of its political, linguistic, and social "construction." As George Lakoff and Sean Illing explain, "People think in terms of conceptual structures called frames and metaphors. It's not just the facts. They have values, and they understand which facts fit into their conceptual framework." We cannot understand something if our brains do not allow it, if is filtered out by those values, beliefs, and prejudices that ultimately constitute us. Conway was in part correct to refer to alternative facts because if you're someone "who shares Trump's worldview, there are certain things that follow from that worldview. In other words, certain things have to be true, or have to be believed, in order to sustain that worldview. The things that aren't actually true but nevertheless preserve that worldview are 'alternative facts' – that's what Conway was getting at, whether she knew it or not."[15]

Predictably, the rise of alternative facts, "post-truth," and "fake news" has been attributed by realists such as Victor Davis Hanson and Maurizio Ferraris to the emergence of postmodern thought. Hanson believes that "academic postmodernism derides facts and absolutes, and insists that there are only narratives and interpretations that gain credence, depending on the power of the story-teller." Ferraris accuses them of having invented "fake news" and holds them responsible for the socio-political consequences.¹⁶ While a greater understanding of the circumstances out of which fake news arises will better equip us to live informed lives, it is necessary to properly characterize postmodernism's contribution:

> The insistence on the primacy of narratives and interpretations does not involve a deriding of facts but an alternative story of their emergence. Postmodernism sets itself against the notion of facts just lying there discrete and independent, and waiting to be described. Instead it argues that fact is the achievement of argument and debate, not a pre-existing entity by whose measure argument can be assessed. Arguments come first; when they are successful, facts follow – at least for a while, until a new round of arguments replaces them with a new set of facts.¹⁷

According to Stanley Fish, "fake news" emerges when data and information are unattached to any interpretation, that is, guidelines, monitors, and filters. When this occurs "what you have are innumerable bits (like Lego) available for assimilation into any project a clever verbal engineer might imagine." Similar to Protestantism, where believers are enjoined to reject merely ecclesiastical authority and go directly to the pure word of God, realism demands a total submission to facts, data, and reality instead of their interpreters. The problem with this distrust of traditional vectors of authority and legitimation (from government agencies and major newspapers to credentialed academics) is that it "leads to the bizarre conclusion that an assertion of fact is more credible if it lacks an institutional source. In this way of thinking, a piece of news originating in a blog maintained by a teenager in a basement in Idaho would be more reliable than a piece of news announced by the anchor of a major network."¹⁸ In the age of alternative facts, facts have also been framed, that is, stripped of all the interpretative, institutional, and social support they once could count on.

As we can see, alternative facts or "fake news" are a consequence not of postmodern philosophers' claiming the indispensable role of interpretation in comprehending the world but rather of the return to order that thinkers of the intellectual dark web are helping impose. The problem of identifying and framing Being, as well as interpretation and emergency, with the present order of entities and thought as a mirror of reality is that freedom is also framed. In order to preserve freedom from external impositions it is necessary to show how these three fundamental concepts are beyond realist frames. This can be done by examining the remains of Being, the anarchic vein of interpretation, and the absence of emergency. The remains of Being disclose how metaphysics, conversation, and truth can be weakened to avoid Being's identification with present entities. And interpretation's anarchic vein can confront this identification through resistances, transgressions, and alternations. The absence of emergency discloses the political effects that emerge from this identification.

These three notions will not only provide the tools for a definition of freedom in the afterword but also respond to Elliot Alderson's uncertainties about being contained in our framed global order. While sometimes he envies those within this order – "What I wouldn't give to be normal. To live in that bubble, the reality of the naïve" – other times he acknowledges through Mr Robot that it is necessary to stay at large – "You're here because you sense something wrong with the world. Something you can't explain, but you know it controls you and everyone you care about. It turns them into slaves. And that *angers you*." The choice belongs to all of us.

Part One

BEING

We find ourselves surveilled and managed to an extraordinary degree, farmed for our personal data, fed consumer goods but discouraged from speaking our minds or doing anything too disruptive in the world, and regularly reminded that racial, sexual, religious and ideological conflict are not closed cases at all. Perhaps we are ready to talk about freedom again – and talking about it politically also means talking about it in our personal lives … Many of our uncertainties about freedom amount to uncertainties about our fundamental Being.

– Sarah Bakewell, *At the Existentialist Café*

The problem of Being is intrinsically bound to the German philosopher Martin Heidegger. He is the thinker who rescued philosophy from Being's oblivion and its misunderstanding as an eternal and unchanging ground for all reality. More than forty years after his death, he continues to influence philosophers, political theorists, and intellectuals across diverse fields. European philosophers such as Jean Paul Sartre, Hannah Arendt, and Slavoj Žižek; Asian thinkers such as Keiji Nishitani, Chen Jiaying, and Yuk Hui; the South American theorist Rodolfo Kusch; and renowned architects, filmmakers, and novelists such as Daniel Libeskind, Terrence Malick, and Tom McCarthy have all carefully studied and were deeply influenced by the German thinker's analysis of human existence and his critique of modern hyper-technological rationalism. Although few would deny that Heidegger is one of the most influential thinkers of the twentieth century, today it is impossible to read him without knowing that he was also a member of the Nazi party, which has chilling effects on the way he is studied and remembered. The recent publication of Heidegger's *Schwarze Hefte* (*Black Notebooks*), which consists of philosophical, political, and personal notes from the early 1930s to the early 1970s, forced readers to confront his dark political views or at least to recognize them.[1]

This publication has received exaggerated attention in books, essays, and articles. Not only did we all already know about his involvement with the Nazi regime and his racist views, but this focus is also an attempt once again to channel his anti-Semitism into the history of Being. This attempt, as Jürgen Habermas said, is absurd.[2] It's part of what David Farrell Krell calls the "Heidegger scandal industry," where publishers take advantage of academics' eagerness to demonstrate that they belong to the good side of history by linking Heidegger's "stupid talk about the international Jewish conspiracy to all the other things that weigh on his thought, distorting and diminishing it, marring it in ways one never can and never should forget."[3] Heidegger's political actions and views should not be ignored or forgotten, but it is important to continue to both read and criticize his philosophy, as has been done with David Hume, who considered black people to be naturally inferior to whites, or Gottlob Frege, who also sympathized with fascism and anti-Semitism.

Although Heidegger, together with Gadamer, Derrida, and Vattimo, is at the centre of this chapter, my goal is not to channel their political views into the history of Being but rather to understand the meaning of Being after the deconstruction of metaphysics. Being's meaning will not only show how partial all previous responses have been but also identify the dominant and oppressive role that metaphysics has upon our interpretation of the world. This probably explains why so many thinkers, from Emmanuel Lévinas to Reiner Schürmann and Catherine Malabou, proposed different conceptions of Being. These interpretations, among other things, are necessary to remind us that science does not have all the answers and that we should look askance at the central role it has acquired in relation to philosophy and other disciplines. Being can help us understand that scientists do "not think in the way thinkers think." Scientific thinkers calculate within framed paradigms, but philosophers' thought explores the frame and the paradigms as well as the products of the sciences. "The trouble," as Gregory Fried explains, "is that science can tell us what human beings are, as collections of atoms or products of evolution since the Big Bang, but science as such can neither tell us who we are nor provide the moral compass for where we should be going, given that we are here." This is why

> we can and should think the question of Being against Heidegger, and perhaps with Plato and those after him, but if we don't think the question at all, we will stagger blindly to our fate. As we persist in fouling our own nest in the relentless quest for power upon power and resource upon resource, as we ramp up the apocalyptic lethality of our weaponry, as the march of technology continues to transform even human nature itself, we will in this coming century have to confront the question, "to be or not to be" – and what does it mean to be human upon this earth? If we cannot feel the force of that question, we won't even get started with an answer.[4]

Heidegger does not believe that physical and life sciences are useless but simply that they are framed within what he called "metaphysics." The sciences (often also philosophy) are metaphysical when they attempt to understand things through eternal entities (whether ideas, God, or the laws of modern physics) and objectively present references. For example, when we ask what something "actually is," such as an apple or an ethical value, the answer is never "this red apple" or "that ethical value I apply" because those are simply temporary examples. The correct answer would be what we consider an apple or ethical value always to be. However, the problem with this response according to Heidegger is that it presupposes an eternal and present entity that will always tell us the truth no matter who and where we are. Instead, as Heidegger explained, truth is not what corresponds to an eternal and objective reality but rather what unfolds to us as human beings in a given space, time, and tradition. This means that our primary encounter with the world is not objective, that is, the experience of a spectator staring at a world, but rather an involved one where things are filled with human meaning.

In a televised interview in 1969 Heidegger told Richard Wisser that the "fundamental thought of my thinking is precisely that Being, or the manifestation [*Offenbarkeit*] of being, *needs* human beings and that, vice versa, human beings are only human beings if they are standing in the manifestation of Being."[5] What Heidegger is trying to point out is what makes human beings different from other beings that are not human: the capacity to "stand" in the manifestation or genuine appearance of Being. This is why he does not believe we exist in the world as pure reason but rather as a "thrown project," that is, an individual with interests, concerns, and expectations. This is probably why Habermas has praised the way Heidegger's "postmetaphysical historicizing" advances the "overcoming of the philosophy of subjectivity ... From today's standpoint, Heidegger's new beginning still presents probably the most profound turning point in German philosophy since Hegel."[6]

Contrary to the traditional tripartition of man into body, soul, and spirit, Heidegger coined the term "Dasein," which is not the world, the subject, or a property of both but the relation, the in-between, which does not arise from the subject's coming together with the world but from its essential features: "thrownness," "fallenness," and, in particular, "existence." "Thrownness" refers to the fact that Dasein always finds itself already in a certain historically conditioned environment, hence, in a world where the space of possibilities is always historically limited. "Fallenness" instead characterizes its existence in the midst of beings that are both Dasein and not Dasein. Existence, which is Dasein's central feature, refers to its potentiality-for-being, "Seinkönnen," since it projects its being upon various possibilities, in particular the phenomenon of the future. It is this essential characteristic that makes Dasein not a rational being but, more profoundly, a relationship to Being upon which humanity must decide if it wants to exist as "a describer of objectivity" or a "interpreter of Being."

The paradigmatic example of the describer of objectivity can be found in Descartes, for whom the world consists of objects that are already there as such even before they are investigated, that is, as if Dasein could only "understand its own being in terms of that being to which it is essentially, continually, and most of all closely related – the 'world' … in terms of what is objectively present."⁷ If this were the case, our thought would only have to re-present objects in search of objective accounts, but such a philosophy would imply that we all have an impossible God's-eye view for which the truth of things exists in the form of a timeless presence. This is why Heidegger could define metaphysics as the "age of the world picture," where the world, truth, and reality are reduced, constituted, and presented as images for practical manipulation.

> According to common opinion, "thinkers" are concerned "only" with "thoughts" and reside amid what is "unreal." On the other hand, practical persons dwell in the "real." What? Is not the practical person the unconditional slave of his mere un-free "thought"? Is not the thinker the only free person, standing free in relation to that which, of all beings, is most a Being?⁸

The difference between "practical persons" and "thinkers" is not meant to point simply toward the so-called unreality of Being but also toward how this same condition is what frees thinkers. Whereas practical persons are framed within a reality they do not control, that is, that conditions their relations, thinkers are free because they stand in a hermeneutic relation with Being whose condition is worn out, almost unreal. This does not mean that the remains of Being are unworthy of thought; on the contrary, it is precisely the worn status of Being that challenges philosophical thought to dwell on the decay, interpret the tradition, and generate more Being. The remains of Being that this chapter will outline in relation to metaphysics, conversation, and truth are meant to disclose how Being is at large, that is, freed from those frames that limit its possibilities.

BEING AND METAPHYSICS

In order to understand the relation of Being and metaphysics it is necessary to explore three phases of thought that constitute the current ontological nature of interpretation. Although these phases are not necessarily chronological, they all respond to a tradition that has been not only deconstructed but also weakened to the point where Being, as Heidegger says, "just counts as the sound of a word for us, a used-up term,"[9] which leaves it the task of hermeneutic philosophy today to interpret these remnants of Being, that is, everything beyond metaphysics. The first phase in the ontology of interpretation is the destruction of Being's metaphysical tradition; the second, the reformulation of the fundamental question of metaphysics; and the third, in the different answers hermeneutic philosophers have given to this question. While Heidegger is the central figure of the first two phases, the third encompasses a number of philosophers (in particular Jacques Derrida and Gianni Vattimo) who contributed in a substantial way not only to our understanding of the relation between Being and metaphysics but also to making hermeneutics the *koiné* of the twenty-first century, as Vattimo reaffirms in his *Essere e dintorni* (*Being and its surroundings*), released in 2018. The goal of this first section is to venture into these three phases in order to understand the condition of Being after metaphysics.

According to Heidegger, Western civilization is sustained by metaphysics because every epoch of Western thought, however different it may be from others, is established in some metaphysics, placed in a definite relationship to an understanding of Being. Even though philosophy has been defined, since the mid-seventeenth century, as "ontology," the study of being as such, its essence was, is, and will always be metaphysical. This is why Jean Grondin stresses that "metaphysics is the insurmountable presupposition of all thought insofar as it carried and supported the project of a universal understanding of the world that inquires into the Being of reason for things."[10]

The term "metaphysics" was coined by an early editor of Aristotle's works who collected under the name of "metaphysics" (*meta*: after/beyond and *physics*: nature) all the works that came after his *Physics*. Despite the fact that metaphysics includes other branches (e.g., cosmology, psychology, and so forth), for Aristotle it was meant to be the *first* philosophy, the philosophy that studied being qua being; the problem here is that by limiting itself to the one-sided, objective, present Being of beings, metaphysics has used beings as the only cause for truth, providing an answer to the question of the Being of beings for civilization at large. But in this way it has skilfully removed from the field of investigation the problem of existence, hence, of Being. Metaphysics is the history of the different formations of Being; in other words, it represents the constitutive essence of philosophy where Being has been left aside in order to concentrate on the (physical, technological, ethical, etc.) manipulation of beings. Those problems that have in common this ontological dimension are metaphysical because they look beyond beings and toward their grounds. But why is it necessary to deconstruct metaphysics?

In one of the most important passages of *Being and Time* (1927), Heidegger explains that the ancient interpretation of the Being of beings was oriented toward the "world" in the broadest sense and that it gained its understanding of Being from time:

> The outward evidence of this is the determination of the meaning of Being as "*parousia*" or "*ousia*," which ontologically and temporally means "presence," "*Anwesenheit*." Beings are grasped in their Being as "presence"; that is to say, they are understood with regard to a definite mode of time, the *present*.[11]

The problem with this determination of Being is that Being was determined by time exclusively as presence, in other words, ignoring the ontological difference. But when the distinction of essence and existence arises it is always the first that prevails, the priority of essence over existence leads to an emphasis on beings, on essence as what factually exists here and now. In this way the original meaning of existence as *physis*, originating or arising, is lost, and Being is set up as the permanent nominal presence. Through this interpretation, metaphysics also becomes the history of the oblivion of Being, that is, of what remains of Being. If the destruction of these layers that cover up the original nature of Being, the layers that metaphysical thinking has constructed, has been undertaken in terms of the history of Being, it is because what is present in its presence became the completion of the extreme possibilities of the oblivion of Being.

As we can see, philosophy must destroy all that covers up the sense of Being, the unproven concepts, the functional context, the structures piled on top of one another that make the sense of Being unrecognizable, in order to reveal hitherto unnoticed possibilities. These structures can be found in the passages in which the question of existence, of the "Being in beings," is touched on or is unconsciously implicit. Heidegger wants to deconstruct these metaphysical categories in order to recognize their negative and positive features, compelling them back to their forgotten inception. It is from this inception that we learn how they dominate, through their grammatical third-person-singular, the configuration of Being. Heidegger, in his course from 1927 gave a very clear indication of the goal of deconstruction in relation to the problem of construction:

> Construction in philosophy is necessarily destruction, that is to say, a de-constructing of traditional concepts carried out in a historical recursion to the tradition. And this is not a negation of the tradition or a condemnation of it as worthless; quite the reverse, it signifies precisely a positive appropriation of tradition. Because destruction belongs to construction, philosophical cognition is essentially at the same time, in a certain sense, historical cognition.[12]

Heidegger undertook this deconstruction of the history of Being in order to destroy the sediment that covers up the original nature of Being, the layers that metaphysical thinking has deposited. This is why the "question of Being attains true concreteness only when we carry out the destructuring of the ontological tradition." If "destructuring of the history of ontology essentially belongs to the formulation of the question of Being and is possible solely within such a formulation," it is because the goal is to achieve clarity not only regarding the concept of Being but also regarding the question, hence, "to reach the point where we can come to terms with it in a controlled fashion."[13] But in order to reformulate the fundamental question of metaphysics it is important to remember that "it is constitutive of the being of Dasein to have, in its very Being, a relation of being to this Being" and how this "relation" must be a "hermeneutical relation" with "respect to bringing tidings, with respect to preserving a message."[14] Although this message obviously is the Being of beings, which is what calls humanity to its essential Being, why did Heidegger emphasize that this relation had to be hermeneutical? This relation must be hermeneutical because it must preserve a message, that is, appropriate Being after metaphysics has been deconstructed. But in what condition is Being after such destruction? Heidegger describes this condition in a lecture delivered at Freiburg in the winter semester of 1941, where in section 11, entitled "Being Is the Most Worn-Out [*abgegriffen*] and at the Same Time the Origin," he says:

> For we lay claim to being everywhere, wherever and whenever we experience beings, deal with them and interrogate them, or merely leave them alone. We need being because we need it in all relations to beings. In this constant and multiple use, Being is in a certain way expended. And yet we cannot say that Being is used up in this expenditure. Being remains constantly available to us. Would we wish to maintain, however, that this use of being, which we constantly rely upon, leaves Being so untouched? Is not Being at least consumed in use? Does not the indifference of the "is," which occurs in all saying, attest to the wornness of what we thus name? Being is certainly not grasped, but it is nevertheless worn-out and thus also "empty"

and "common." Being is the most worn-out. Being stands everywhere and at each moment in our understanding as what is most self-understood. It is thus the most worn-out coin with which we constantly pay for every relation to beings, without which payment no relation to beings as beings would be allotted us.[15]

Heidegger's weak determination of Being expresses both the objective and subjective genitive of Being because there is nothing to Being as such; Being is "worn-out" and "needs man for its revelation, preservation and formation."[16] Given that "worn" is the participle of "wear," meaning "spent," affected," or "exhausted" by long use, "worn-out" becomes something that is being used to threadbareness, valuelessness, or uselessness. The end of the destruction of metaphysics blends with the end of the search for Being because philosophy, after having retrieved the question of Being, recognizes how we are left only with the many different interpretations, descriptions, and remains of Being framed within metaphysics. Even though Dasein must be the "guardianship" of Being at all times, Heidegger emphasizes that Being is never "used up in this expenditure," giving Being priority over Dasein. This is also why in his response to Jean-Paul Sartre he stressed that "nous sommes sur un plan où il y a principalement l'Etre [we are precisely in a situation where principally there is Being]."[17]

Heidegger's destruction of metaphysics did not leave it "worn-out to the point of complete exhaustion and disparagement" but rather served to disclose its remnants. This is particularly significant because the excluded middle between Being and Nothingness in the fundamental question of metaphysics ("why are there beings at all instead of nothing?") ends by favouring Being since it is Being that first "lets every Being as such originate. Being first lets every Being be, that means to spring loose and away, to be a Being, and as such to be itself."[18] Philosophy, and now also hermeneutics, does not seek which side is correct but rather the condition, amount, or state of Being. In sum, in order to think Being independently of metaphysics, without beings, in its actual worn-out state, it is necessary to modify the fundamental metaphysical question so as to question Being after its destruction in terms of remnants. As surprising as this might seem, Heidegger elaborated this new question in *Introduction to Metaphysics*:

> As the fundamental question of metaphysics, we ask: "Why are there beings at all instead of nothing?" In this fundamental question there already resonates the prior question: how is it going with Being? What do we mean by the words "to be," Being? In our attempt to answer, we run into difficulties. We grasp at the un-graspable. Yet we are increasingly engaged by beings, related to beings, and we know about ourselves "as beings." Being now just counts as the sound of a word for us, a used-up term. If this is all we have left, then we must at least attempt to grasp this last remnant of a possession. This is why we asked: how is it going with the word Being?[19]

According to Richard Polt and Gregory Fried, who brilliantly translated this important book, "Wie steht es um das Sein?" "could be translated more colloquially as 'What is the status of Being?' or even 'What about Being?' We have kept the German in order to preserve Heidegger's various plays on standing."[20] Although I agree that there isn't a great difference in meaning between the two formulations, I've decided to translate both versions as "How is it going with Being?" because this, as Charles Guignon rightly puts it, "has a colloquial, almost slangy ring to it,"[21] which confirms that Being now appears as something weak "from out of which stem all beings and even their possible annihilation."[22]

Heidegger raised this question ("how is it going with Being?") out from the fundamental question of metaphysics ("Why are there beings at all instead of nothing?") because Being is not a present-at-hand fact but "the fundamental happening, the only ground upon which historical Dasein is granted in the midst of beings that are opened up as a whole." If this were not the case, then Being could be opposed to Nothing within the traditional metaphysical question, ignoring the history of Being. However, as we've seen, Being cannot be opposed to something. Although it appears as an empty word with an evanescent meaning, it still proves to be the worthiest of questioning because it "is the most worn-out and at the same time the origin." As an origin, Being is the power that still today sustains and dominates all our relations to beings, and it must be experienced anew in the full breadth of its possible essence if we want to set our historical Dasein to work; after all, as Heidegger points out, the "essence of Being is intimately linked to the question of who the human being is."[23]

Before venturing into the different answers philosophers have given to this question it is important to emphasize how after its destruction we have to settle down within the language of metaphysics because it is something we cannot overcome in the sense of *überwunden*, defeating and leaving it behind, but only in the sense of *verwindung*, recovering, twisting, or incorporating.

As Hans-Georg Gadamer explained, when Heidegger "modified the overcoming ('*Überwindung*') of metaphysics and replaced it with a coming to terms with ('*Verwindung*') metaphysics,"[24] he was primarily trying to highlight how philosophy can never totally and completely cut loose from its historical heritage. This is why Gadamer also believes "that there can never be 'philosophy' without metaphysics. And yet philosophy is perhaps only philosophy when it leaves metaphysical thinking and sentence logic behind it!"[25] But how can this take place? According to Gadamer the goal of Heidegger's destruction was "to let the concept speak again in its interwovenness in living language" and had "nothing to do with obscure talk of origins and of the original."[26] Contrary to other interpreters of Heidegger's destruction of metaphysics, Gadamer does not believe it was meant to point back to a mysterious origin, an *arché*, or to repudiate this history but to "recover" from metaphysics. This "recovery" is meant to set thought free from framing powers or, which is the same, language from logic. For Gadamer there is "no ultimate language of metaphysics" because language is not only "the house of Being," as Heidegger stressed, but also "the house of the human being, a house where one lives, which one furnishes, and where one encounters oneself, or oneself in others." If Being is on the way to language for Gadamer it's because language's nature is conversational and only through conversation can Being be understood since it comes into language in conversation and not the other way around.

If it is impossible to surpass metaphysics without presupposing it, then "overcoming is worthy only when we think about incorporation."²⁷ Hence, to overcome metaphysics means to incorporate it, to appropriate it, but if metaphysics and its question become something we cannot eliminate by answering the question, then philosophy finally becomes an "appropriation," an appropriation of what remains from the destruction of the history of Being. This is why for Heidegger hermeneutics is not meant to take

> cognizance of something and having knowledge about it, but rather an existential knowing, i.e., a Being [*ein Sein*]. It speaks from out of interpretation and for the sake of it … As far as I am concerned, if this personal comment is permitted, I think that hermeneutics is not philosophy at all, but in fact something preliminary which runs in advance of it and has its own reasons for being: what is at issue in it, what it all comes to, is not to become finished with it as quickly as possible, but rather to hold out in it as long as possible … It wishes only to place an object which has fallen into forgetfulness before today's philosophers for their "well-disposed consideration."²⁸

If a regard for metaphysics still prevails even in the intention to overcome metaphysics, then hermeneutics is the appropriate candidate to cease all overcoming and leave metaphysics to itself. In this way hermeneutic philosophy becomes a "happening that must at all times work out Being for itself anew."²⁹ Working out Being anew is the essential obligatory task of Dasein because if there were no indeterminate meaning of Being, or if we did not understand what this meaning signified, there would be no language at all. Dasein is distinguished by the fact that in its very Being, Being is an issue for it, and mostly because through its comprehension it becomes the manifestation of Being. The task is always a matter of naming Being, which is not a thing but a verb. In other words, if "our essence would not stand within the power of language, then all beings would remain closed off to us – the beings that we ourselves are, no less than the beings that we are not."³⁰ The fact that Being by now just counts as "a used-up," "worn-out" term for us, that "this is all we have left," and that we must at least attempt to grasp this "last remnant of a possession," signifies that Being remains philosophy's main concern, especially after being destroyed, because it becomes unpresentable, indeterminable, and ungraspable. Heidegger's destruction did not destroy but set us free into the remains of Being.

There are a number of philosophers who have not only "work[ed] out Being for itself anew," as Heidegger requested after his destruction of metaphysics, but also proposed weak conceptions of Being, against the foundationalism of earlier metaphysics. Although not all of them declare themselves hermeneutic philosophers, they all share the need to apply the new fundamental question – how is it going with Being? – in order to understand the way that Being occurs today. These worn-out interpretations of Being indicate how metaphysics cannot be ignored or overcome but only twisted or surpassed. I will briefly outline Derrida's and Vattimo's remnants of Being in order to emphasize why Being's worn-out condition suggests a point of departure for hermeneutics rather than its point of arrival.

Derrida followed Heidegger's preference for a "coming to terms with ('*Verwindung*') metaphysics" rather than its "overcoming ('*Überwindung*')" through the idea of traces or, as he preferred to call it, "the treasury of traces." Philosophy "always reappropriates for itself the discourse that de-limits it"³¹ because we always conduct our activities in an understanding of Being that we do not comprehend; in other words, philosophy is delimited by its own question, which comprehends (since we always have a vague understanding of Being) but cannot fix conceptually through communicative meaning. "It remains," says Derrida, "that the meaning of these 'limits' is given to us only on the basis of the question of the meaning of Being."

The French thinker's goal was to explain how the limitation of the sense of Being within the field of presence (that is, Western metaphysics) was produced through the domination of a linguistic form "*derivative* with regard to difference," as well as to question "what constitutes our history and what produced transcendentality itself."[32] This is why for Derrida the sense of Being is not transcendental or trans-epochal, but "a determined signifying trace." The ontological difference and its grounds are not simply originary but also derivative with regard to what he calls "*différance*," "differance." Derrida has used a graphical intervention with the French word *différence* (difference), by substituting the *a* for the *e* and producing a modification that remains purely graphic: "it is read, or it is written, but it cannot be heard."[33] But why is this useful for Derrida's deconstruction?

This operation "marks the *movement* of this unfolding"[34] of the ontological difference, and it allows him to refer to an order (of the trace) that no longer belongs to sensibility nor intelligibility, to the ideality that is not fortuitously affiliated with the objectivity of metaphysical understanding; in other words, this is an order that resists the founding "opposition of philosophy between sensible and intelligible."[35] *Différance* is not only what in the presence of the present does not present itself, hence, a way to name the trace that does not present itself but also the same condition that exposes what is present because

> *the (pure) trace is differance*. It does not depend on any sensible plentitude, audible or visible, phonic or graphic. It is, on the contrary, the condition of such a plenitude. Although it *does not exist*, although it is never a *being-present* outside of all plenitude, its possibility is by rights anterior to all that one calls sign (signified/signifier, content/expression, etc.), concept or operation, motor or sensory. This differance is therefore not more sensible than intelligible and it permits the articulation of signs among themselves within the same abstract order – a phonic or graphic text for example – or between two orders of expression.[36]

The trace serves Derrida as a way to overcome the very condition of the illusion of the presence of Being, which presupposes that any being, element, or concept can be present in and of itself, that is, referring only to itself. If "no element can function as a sign without referring to another element which itself is not simply present," then there "are only, everywhere, differences and traces of traces."[37] Each being that appears on the scene of presence, just like the signified concept, is always related to something other than itself or inscribed, as Derrida explains, in a "system within which it refers to the other, to other concepts, by means of the systematic play of differences. Such a play, *différance*, is thus no longer simply a concept, but rather the possibility of conceptuality." Experience, for Derrida, is always an experience of trace.

By deconstructing the originary presence of Being, naming and individuating the nonpresent difference (*différance*) from the ontological difference as "something that remains without remaining, which is neither present nor absent, which destroys itself, which is totally consumed, which is a remainder without remainder," Derrida has responded to our question: How is it going with Being? He has named the remains of Being "traces," "cinders," and "ashes,"[38] creating a new "order" that does not belong anymore to Being as presence, although "it transports it" and "includes ontotheology."[39]

While Derrida has not directly referred to the "weakness" of his "trace" in relation to metaphysics, Vattimo's Being is explicitly understood as a weakened concept. This weakness is the result not only of Being's condition after its destruction but also of the impossibility of answering the fundamental question of metaphysics. If we have not been able to answer this question once and for all, Vattimo specifies, it's not "because of its force ... but because of its weakness."[40] This is why "if Being had a strong reason to be, then metaphysics would have significance, would have strength. But as things are, Being ... is historical and casual, happened and happening."[41] As we can see, Vattimo's Being is an event, an *Ereignis*. This term was first used by Heidegger in *Contributions to Philosophy* (1936) to mark a new ontological approach that excludes all essentialist views of Being.

Heidegger's "coming to terms" or "twisting" (*Verwindung*) of metaphysics in Vattimo's thought is fully integrated into an interpretation of Being as an "event" and philosophy as "weak thought." The Italian thinker believes that "what is ahead of philosophy as its goal, after deconstructionism, is a labor of stitching things back together, of reassembly."[42] However, the event that takes place through "weak thought" is the result not of the destruction of metaphysics but rather of the historical acknowledgment that this destruction was meant to weaken Being's objective presence. This is why for Vattimo we belong to this same destruction, that is, to "a philosophy of 'decline,' a philosophy which sees what is constitutive of Being not as the fact of its prevailing, but of the fact of its disappearing."[43] In this condition, Being becomes an event because philosophy no longer corresponds to the Platonic agenda of understanding Being through the Eternal but rather seeks to do so through its own history; that is, it redirects itself toward history. Nonetheless, this is only possible if Being and event are fused together so that Being derives not from Being "as it is" but from Being viewed as the product of a history of formulations, deconstructions, and interpretations that "are 'givens' of destiny understood as a process of trans-mission. They are points of reference we keep encountering each time we engage in thinking here and now."[44] If Being for Vattimo consists in a trans-mission, in the forwarding and destiny (*Ueber-lieferung* and *Ge-schick*) of a series of echoes, linguistic resonances, and messages coming from the past and from others in the form of events, why is hermeneutics the philosophical position that responds to this process?

Vattimo finds that hermeneutics presents itself as the most appropriate form to the "thinking that corresponds to Being as *event*" because it is a philosophical position that grasps Being's vocation of giving itself as the truth of human language. This is why the "eventual" nature of Being is nothing but "the disclosure of historico-linguistic horizons within which beings (things, men, etc.) come into presence."[45] In this manner Being never really *is* but sends itself, is on the way, transmits itself through the horizon of language.

> The comprehensive historical horizon, which supports the varied permutations of historical horizons, is nothing other than the horizon of language. And just as much as it belongs

to history, man belongs to language rather than possessing language as a tool. Thus every formalization of language, which claims to establish the limits and modalities of languages by means of rigorous conventions, always moves within an already existing language that makes it possible.[46]

Having said this, one might think with Gadamer that language is something bigger than or prior to Being, but, on the contrary, it is an event of Being itself, an "eventuality" that indicates how everything we see as a structure, essence, or theorem is an event, a historical aperture or disclosure of Being. In this way, Being presupposes this disclosure, which is not an object of philosophical research but rather that into which it is always–already thrown.

So for Vattimo Being is not what endures, what is and cannot not be – as Parmenides, Plato, and Aristotle would have it – but only what becomes because it "becomes" from the ontological difference, which was central also to Derrida. What becomes comes to life and dies and for that reason has a history, a permanence of its own in its concatenated multiplicity of meanings and interpretations.

Even though Derrida and Vattimo recognize that hermeneutics originally was a theory that legitimized its interpretations by demonstrating it could reconstruct the history of certain events, they are more interested in indicating how it can also be an interpretation from within, that is, from what it always–already belongs to "since this belonging is the very condition for the possibility of receiving messages."[47] However, as we have seen, this belonging is nothing else than the remains of Being or, in Derrida's and Vattimo's words, the trace and event of Being.

While there are a number of other philosophers (such as Jean-Luc Nancy, Giorgio Agamben, and Alain Badiou) who have responded to Heidegger's request to "work out Being for itself anew" in order to "grasp its last remnant of a possession" through the "new fundamental question of philosophy,"[48] it is Derrida and Vattimo who have given hermeneutics the necessary tools for future generations to take on this task. This task will prevent philosophy from falling back into metaphysics and will also grant it access to history, that is, allow it to become futural because, as Heidegger once said, the "possibility of access to history is grounded in the possibility according to which any specific present understands how to be futural. This is the first principle of all hermeneutics. It says something about the Being of Dasein, which is historicity itself."[49] In sum, hermeneutic philosophy becomes the key for the future because interpretation is, in itself, a response to a message, an articulated response to the remains of Being, which are never a static essence but rather always at large.

BEING AND CONVERSATION

Contrary to a dialogue, in which at least one of the interlocutors knows where it is headed, in a conversation we are also always at large. The relation between Being and conversation is vital for the recognition that there is no goal in hermeneutic philosophy besides keeping open the remains of Being. This is why among the most important consequences of Heidegger's destruction of Being as presence, in addition to the overcoming of metaphysics and the elevation of hermeneutics to the centre of philosophical concern, is the weakening of Being to its own remains. While few Heideggerian scholars consider the German master's philosophical destruction as a weakening of Being, most contemporary hermeneutic philosophers agree that he was the first to have given ontological import to hermeneutics. Hermeneutics for Heidegger, as Michael Bowler and Ingo Farin recently explained in a book dedicated to the German thinker's philosophy of interpretation, "goes beyond merely academic philosophical concerns, reaching to the core of our being and of being as such."[50]

For such authors as Nancy Holland, Georgia Warnke, and Jeff Malpas, philosophical interpretation has become not only a philosophical problem in itself but also the ground to start overcoming the division between analytic and continental philosophy. Most contemporary analytic philosophies (such as John Searle or Barry Smith) continue to restrict ontology to a scientific focus from the empiricist tradition. And continental philosophers (such as Crina Gschwandtner or Jean-Luc Marion) firmly maintain the objectivist intentionality of their phenomenologist tradition. But today, more than half a century after the publication of Gadamer's *Truth and Method* (1960), hermeneutics has the opportunity to leave aside these traditional metaphysical aspirations for indubitable knowledge.

Philosophical hermeneutics is not yet another variation of the antagonism between continental philosophy and analytical philosophy. Rather, it represents the dissolution of such a division in the discipline, where language is not used to represent reality but to help break "the crust of convention of the epistemology industry" and continue the "conversation of humankind" as John Dewey and Richard Rorty would say. While a new interchangeable framework already has begun to take shape in the fusing together of problems from both traditions in such authors as Marianne Janack, Robert Brandom, and John McDowell, this same framework will not become the thought of the twenty-first century until it overcomes metaphysics in a productive way. However, if hermeneutics can present itself as the postmetaphysical thought of the twenty-first century it is not only because its classic practitioners (Schleiermacher, Dilthey, and Nietzsche) have broken ground for it and others from both traditions (Ernst Tugendhat, Sam Wheeler, Tina Fernandes Botts) have developed it but also because it has become the most appropriate response to Heidegger's destruction of metaphysics. However, this has occurred only because hermeneutics has left its conservative focus on dialogue and become a progressive conversational philosophy where success, as Rorty pointed out, is measured by "horizons fused rather than problems solved, or even by problems dissolved."[51] More than a philosophical position in search of Being's origins, hermeneutics, through Vattimo and Rorty, has become a system of thought that aims to disclose Being's remains.

My aim in this section is to show that Heidegger's destruction of metaphysics together with the ontological effects of hermeneutics will result in "conversation," which is a concept Gadamer placed at the centre of his philosophy. Gadamer championed conversation not simply because it's something one gets "caught up in" or where the interlocutors "can lose themselves"⁵² but primarily because it's the process of coming to an understanding. When "our own concepts threaten to become rigid" and we become unable to understand others, the process of a conversation can "break down resistance in ourselves"⁵³ to listening. Similar to an event, a conversation has a sprit of its own that expresses itself through twists and turns such that one does not know in advance how it will conclude.

Although Gadamer was the first to stress conversation's ontological nature, it is Rorty and Vattimo who interpret its post-metaphysical implications, that is, comprehend it as something "weak" "in comparison to scientific inquiry."⁵⁴ As a remnant of Being, conversation will become not only an appropriate effect of Heidegger's destruction of metaphysics but also, as Vattimo has emphasized, "what interpretation can generate," that is, "Being, new senses of experience, new ways for the world to announce itself."⁵⁵

Before venturing into conversation as a remnant of Being, it should be pointed out that Reiner Schürmann and Jacques Derrida are among the few philosophers who have granted destruction the central role it deserves in Heidegger's thought. Derrida practised deconstruction as his postmetaphysical system, and Schürmann indicated that such practice may only occur in the "absence of foundations." Although they are both original interpreters of Heidegger's destruction of metaphysics, only Vattimo and Rorty have inherited its ontological consequences and, through hermeneutics, used them as a way to overcome metaphysics: the first by interpreting destruction as the weakening of Being into its remains and the second indicating the conversational nature of such Being. Both Vattimo and Rorty not only radically developed Heidegger's destruction into "weak thought" but also followed the German master's most innovative request: to "work out Being for itself anew."⁵⁶ Having said this, it should not come as a surprise that these are among the few interpreters of Heidegger who tend to reject the so-called turn that the German master supposedly went through after the publication of *Being and Time*, that is, from an analysis of Dasein's being to a consideration of the history of the epochs of Being. Those interpreters who emphasize this turn also tend to consider *Being and Time* the only text where Heidegger produces innovative philosophy, when in fact the analysis of Being is a constant throughout his writings.

However, Heidegger's philosophy of Being was also a progressive development that allowed him to respond to the destruction he imposed on Being. A confirmation of this can be found in his preface to the seventh German edition (1953) of *Being and Time*, where Heidegger claims that for an elucidation of the question of Being, "the reader may refer [to] my *Introduction to Metaphysics*."[57] While this text is only a lecture course he delivered at the University of Freiburg in the summer semester of 1935, it is also the first one Heidegger chose to present for general publication in 1953. This is not only the most significant of Heidegger's texts after *Being and Time* but also the essential explication of *Being and Time*. If in the 1927 magnum opus the central concern was the question of Being, it is in this text that this same question is finally "elucidated." Also, the destruction did not begin in *Being and Time* but rather in his courses in Freiburg and Marburg of 1923 entitled "Ontology – the Hermeneutics of Facticity" which continued throughout his volumes on Nietzsche and in his notes in *Contributions to Philosophy*. Throughout these texts, Being was both a constant problem and a progressive response, adapting not only to its own destruction but also to the new fundamental questions ("how is it going with Being?") this brought about. In sum, "destruction" is not an isolated word within Heidegger's works; rather, as Vattimo has emphasized, it stands for the totality of a path to follow: the history of the weakening of Being.

Heidegger probably borrowed the term *Destruktion* from Luther's *Heidelberger Disputation* of 1518, where the church reformer used it to dismantle institutional theology in the name of the authenticity of the evangelical message. Nevertheless, contrary to the theologian's intentions, Heidegger was not looking for authentic or original Being but rather seeking to free it from too objective an interpretation, which limited its existential possibilities through excluding binary polarities such as Being vs.

nothingness, truth vs. error, or mind vs. matter. These polarities arose from understanding the objects of the world independently of our existence, that is, as things in themselves. However, if this were the case and we only had to re-present these objects in their timeless presence, that is, give scientific objective accounts, then our Being would become an object like any other. Instead, as Heidegger immediately explained in *Being and Time*, we have a relation to our Being that is called "existence" because it is a self-relationship, hence a Being-relationship: the "ontic Dasein distinction of Dasein lies in the fact that it *is* ontological."[58] From the start, destruction was not a matter of finding the true Being but rather of venturing into a historico-theoretical inquiry of the Being of beings.

A confirmation of this comes from Heidegger's criticism of the conception of truth as correspondence – "*veritas est adaequatio rei et intellectus*" – since it presupposes the idea of an original Being that would work as an insurmountable first principle. Although this traditional theory of truth is already a consequence of the metaphysical interpretation of Being, that is, where the distinction between the essence and existence of things went forgotten, Heidegger did not criticize it in order to find a truer theory but rather because, as Otto Pöggeler explained, he was looking for a "different conceptual platform." Pöggeler was the first to notice this and recalls how already "in his first lectures Heidegger put forward the demand to take into account the practical and religious truth together with the theoretical one."[59] This is why Heidegger's understanding of truth as disclosedness was not meant for a particular discipline or cultural paradigm but rather for thought in general, that is, for the forgotten space between Being and beings: the ontological difference. There is an interesting testimonial by Gadamer that shows how, for Heidegger, the ontological difference was not something produced by the philosopher.

> I still recall quite clearly how, in Marburg, the young Heidegger developed this concept of the "ontological difference" in the sense of the difference between being and beings, between *ousia* and *on*. One day, as Gerhard Krüger and I accompanied Heidegger home, one of the two of us raised the question of

what, then, the significance of this ontological distinction was, how and when one must make this distinction. I will never forget Heidegger's answer: Make? Is the ontological difference something that must be made? That is a misunderstanding. This difference is not something introduced by the philosopher's thinking so as to distinguish between being and beings.⁶⁰

While Heidegger's ontological difference can be interpreted as an outcome of the destruction of metaphysics, it can be "experienced as something forgotten only ... if it has left a trace."⁶¹ This is why it is not something introduced by the philosopher in order to arrest the investigation; rather, as he specified in *Being and Time*, it is the "point *of departure* for the ontological problematic." The meaning of philosophy, as he explained in 1956, should not be sought in

> historical assertions about the definitions of philosophy but through conversing with that which has been handed down to us as the Being of being. This path to the answer to our question is not a break with history, no repudiation of history, but is an adoption and transformation of what has been handed down to us. Such an adoption of history is what is meant by the term "destruction." ... Destruction does not mean destroying but dismantling, liquidating, putting to one side the merely historical assertions about the history of philosophy. Destruction means – to open our ears, to make ourselves free for what speaks to us in tradition as the Being of being.⁶²

Heidegger's "destruction" was not meant to discover the ontological difference but rather to move us into such "conversing," that is, letting Being speak to us through its tradition and thought. This implies, first of all, that philosophy since Plato has not only been a "forgetfulness of Being" but also an expression of Being's remains. If Heidegger repeatedly insisted that "es gibt Sein [there is Being]" it is because Being is an event that overcomes all metaphysical or descriptive inquiries that would eventually fulfill our needs. For this reason, rather than the truth of Being, we are left with the remains of Being, since to "remain," explained Heidegger, means "not to disappear, thus, to presence."[63] In other words, remains are those worn-out fragments that are not only left after use but also survive. In this way, the enduring Being for Heidegger is not the strongest but, on the contrary, the worn-out, weakest, and vaporous word of which there is nothing as such and which is never exhausted in the present of its inscription.

Heidegger, by stressing that "Being remains constantly available to us," is not only foreshadowing its condition ("worn-out") but also specifying how the thought of Being, that is, metaphysics in general, cannot be *overcome* (*Überwindung*) but only surpassed, come to terms with (*Verwindung*.) As I have said, while *Überwindung* refers to a complete abandonment of the problem, *Verwindung* instead alludes to the way one surpasses a major disappointment not by forgetting it but by coming to terms with it or, as Heidegger said, "what happens when, in the human realm, one works through grief or pain."[64] While this is not the only passage where Heidegger exposes the state of Being after metaphysics, it does indicate that it is not what Being is but how it remains that is essential for philosophy after its destruction. In other words, the end of metaphysics blends with the end of the search for Being's presence since philosophy, after having retrieved the question of Being through the destruction of its own tradition, recognizes that we are left only with its remains. In this condition the excluded middle of Being vs nothingness in the traditional question of metaphysics ("why are there beings at all instead of nothing?") finishes by favouring Being since, as Heidegger said, it is Being that first "lets every Being as such originate. Being first lets every Being be, that means to spring loose and away, to be a Being, and as such to be itself."[65]

As we can see, philosophy after the destruction of metaphysics does not depend anymore on the possibility that one choice in a polarity might be correct but rather on the condition of Being, which is to say, its remains. Although in *Introduction to Metaphysics* one cannot find the term "worn-out," Heidegger does comment that Nietzsche is "entirely right when he calls the 'highest concepts' such as Being 'the final wisp of evaporating reality.'"

Being is no longer a present-at-hand fact but "the fundamental happening, the only ground upon which historical Dasein is granted in the midst of beings that are opened up as a whole." This text is a confirmation that Heidegger's destruction of metaphysics does not imply the end of metaphysics, that is, of the relation of thinking to Being or of subject to object, but only the admission that when "we determine how Being and thinking stand opposed to each other, we are working with a well-worn schema" that we cannot overcome. Heidegger concluded this book by calling for philosophy to "work out Being for itself anew" because after its destruction Being cannot be found or discovered but must be incorporated, appropriated, or interpreted. This is why several years later Heidegger in "Time and Being" would clarify how a "regard for metaphysics still prevails even in the intention to overcome metaphysics. Therefore, our task, is to cease all overcoming, and leave metaphysics to itself."[66]

Although Heidegger gave several names for this task (*An-Denken*, dwelling, appropriation), they all belong to the new fundamental question of philosophy ("How is it going with Being?"), which is an invitation to continue to think after metaphysics. Now, the word "after" alludes not only to the German term *Nachdenken*, the "thinking that follows," but also to "following upon," to the "follower of Being." To engage in *Denken*, thinking, is not to analyze but to attend to or remember Being since the *Bauen*, to build, which comes after the destruction of something, does not point to the notion of a novel construction but to *Hegen*, conservation, preservation, and custodianship. This is why philosophy after the destruction has become a response, an answer to the history of the various events of Being that have been handed down to us through the language of Being. In contrast to the Cartesian, phenomenological, realist attitude, which holds as the task of the philosopher grasping what is in front of him, the postmetaphysical philosopher becomes a listener, a respondent to the remains of Being in order to establish a relation of "audition." Instead of a philosophical description of the origin, presence, or truth of Being, philosophy after the destruction of metaphysics becomes an interpretation of Being's remains.

While Heidegger never named hermeneutics as the thought he was trying to articulate after the destruction of metaphysics, there are several indications in his writings that reveal it as where his thought was tending. For example, in the course of 1923 he explained that hermeneutics is not meant to achieve knowledge about things "but rather an existential knowing, i.e., a Being." In this way, the philosophical problem for hermeneutics is not to describe Being as accurately as possible but rather to guard, hold, and interpret its remains. This is also why Heidegger believes that hermeneutics is not a philosophy at all but rather the interpretation of Being, "which has fallen into forgetfulness before today's philosophers for their well-disposed consideration."[67] In addition, discussing *Being and Time* with Tomio Tezuka in the 1950s, Heidegger continued to regard hermeneutics as the thought that could call humanity to its essential Being, that is, "to bring together what is concealed within the old."[68] As we can see, Heidegger's interest in hermeneutics went beyond the traditional theories of interpretation that provided the criteria for understanding what a text, event, or author really meant; he was interested in its ontological effects.

I believe that the ontological effects of interpretation consist in Being, that is, generating further remains of Being. But how can interpretation generate Being if, as I said earlier, "es gibt Sein," or "il y a de l'être" always already? Actually, it is just because Being is already there that it can be generated through interpretation and not created from a void. After all, the ontological difference allows us to understand Being as the horizon within which we live instead of an independent realm to be grasped. More than a philosophical position in search of Being's origins, hermeneutics has become the postmetaphysical thought that Heidegger was looking for to "work out Being for itself anew."

Rorty and Vattimo, as we will see in the next chapter, are among the few contemporary philosophers who have conceived hermeneutics as the appropriate system of thought for approaching the end of metaphysics. Both philosophers have resisted their philosophical traditions, respectively, analytic and continental philosophy, not to search for another philosophical position but rather against this same search. What binds them together is their common interest in leaving metaphysics aside, as Heidegger requested, and also in transforming philosophy's obsession with truth in favour of a continuation of the conversation. Rorty and Vattimo have exposed, through their postmetaphysical hermeneutics, that "different conceptual platform" that Heidegger was looking for in order to take into "account," as Pöggeler explained, "the practical and religious truth together with the theoretical one," that is, "weak thought."

"Weak thought" is a term Vattimo formulated in the early 1980s and that Rorty endorsed soon afterward.[69] It invites analytic and continental philosophers to abandon their metaphysical claims to global descriptions of the world. In this idea, philosophical, religious, and scientific truth are not only circumscribed to their own historical paradigms but, most of all, conceived of as contingent effects of their historical paradigms. The fact that their truth claims are weakened should not be interpreted as a failure but as a possibility for emancipation, that is, for independence from an objectivity that restricts horizons. Vattimo, by suggesting that Heidegger's destruction be read as the weakening of the structures of metaphysics, and Rorty, by indicating how the value of philosophy is now "a matter of its relation not to a subject-matter but to the rest of the conversation of humankind,"[70] have overcome metaphysics and emphasize its inevitable continuation in hermeneutics. Weak thought is the common position within which Vattimo and Rorty's hermeneutics may operate without falling back in metaphysics and by generating new Being through its own effects. As Vattimo explains, interpretation

> generates Being, new senses of experience, new ways for the world to announce itself, which are not only other than the ones announced "before." Rather, they join the latter in a sort of *discursus* whose logic (also in the sense of Logos) consists precisely in the continuity ... Ontological hermeneutics replaces the metaphysics of presence with a concept of Being that is essentially constituted by the feature of dissolution.

Being gives itself not once and for all as a simple presence; rather, it occurs as announcement and grows into the interpretations that listen and correspond (to Being).[71]

Vattimo's ontological hermeneutics is possible only within the remains of Being, that is, as a continuation, not a discovery. Whereas descriptions represent Being, interpretations generate Being. However, this generation is not autonomous but part of the continuity of that metaphysics that we cannot overcome. What is made manifest is not Being but the remains of Being, those effects of Being that spring only from the ontological difference. Although "effects," from Latin "*effectus*," "performance" or "accomplishment," can be used for various functions, as in John L. Austin's speech acts, it is here understood against hermeneutics' traditional search for causes, origins, or truth. This is why Vattimo defined hermeneutics "as the philosophical theory of the interpretative character of every experience of truth" and the only one that is "lucid about itself as no more than an interpretation."[72]

It is for these same reasons that Rorty decided to endorse hermeneutics, which he did not consider a philosophical position but rather the "expression of hope that the cultural space left by the demise of epistemology will not be filled."[73] Similarly, for Rorty philosophical hermeneutics is not just a defence of human sciences, a challenger of scientific method, or an opponent of analytic philosophy but rather "what we get when we are no longer epistemological."[74] If hermeneutics were just another discipline or position, that is, the discovery that there are different perspectives on the world, it would presuppose a conception of truth as the objective mirror of how things are, which Rorty wants to avoid. Avoiding this metaphysical notion of truth directed Rorty toward Heidegger's hermeneutics, which is more about the effects than the origins of truth.

So Heidegger, Vattimo, and Rorty did not see in hermeneutics a new method for philosophy or an alternative way for philosophy to elucidate texts, represent reality, or translate communication but, on the contrary, a thought beyond these alternatives. Against the architects of hermeneutics (Pareyson, Gadamer, and Ricoeur), Rorty and Vattimo have redirected hermeneutics to respond to Heidegger's destruction of metaphysics and its consequences. The aim of weak thought's hermeneutics is to continue generating new meaning within the words of our language.

Although neither Heidegger, Vattimo, nor Rorty ever coupled Being and conversation, this idea responds not only to the destruction of Being as presence but also to the new fundamental question of philosophy: "How is it going with Being?" In order to justify this thesis, it is necessary to always recall the difference between dialogue and conversation already elucidated, in other words, between Gadamer's conservative hermeneutics and weak thought's progressive hermeneutics.

While Rorty and Vattimo gave Gadamer's philosophical hermeneutics great significance throughout their writings, they both hew much closer to Heidegger's postmetaphysical thought than to Gadamer's hermeneutic theory. This is confirmed in both Georgia Warnke and Jean Grondin, two distinguished interpreters of Gadamer who have accused Rorty and Vattimo of misreading the German master's hermeneutics. Warnke reminds Rorty that Gadamer does not replace truth with edification but rather "sees hermeneutics as an assessment of validity claims."[75] Grondin goes even further in considering Vattimo's nihilistic interpretation of Gadamer's famous thesis ("Being that can be understood is language") a "form of linguistic relativism"[76] that cannot be found in the German master. Both Warnke and Grondin are correct, and they find a confirmation of their criticism in Heidegger, who considered hermeneutical philosophy "Gadamer's business," in other words, radically different from the existential thought he was looking for.[77] However, this difference comes not from hermeneutics' interpretative function but rather from Gadamer's inherent metaphysical search for truth through dialogue. For Gadamer, "truth" is a goal that can be reached through dialogue; for hermeneutics, "conversation" is a way to avoid "asking the question of what is or is not real."[78]

Although Gadamer did not pursue Heidegger's destruction of metaphysics, he did follow his insistence on language (as the house of Being) in order to specify the fundamental role language plays in our existence. Language becomes a "we" where we are all assigned a place in relation to one another in order to understand because "Being that can be understood is language." Language is the "element in which we live, as fishes live in water ... in linguistic interaction we call it a conversation."[79] However, there is a fundamental difference within this linguistic interaction that must pointed out.

The German words *Gespräch*, *Dialog*, and *Unterhaltung* should be literally translated as "discussion," "dialogue," and "conversation," but most translators of Gadamer's works have rightly translated *Gespräch* as "conversation." This is not because of linguistic arbitrariness but because of a philosophical demand implicit in its meaning. *Gespräch* does not allude to something programmed in advance under the direction of a subject matter, wherein the partners leave aside their particular prejudices. On the contrary, a genuine *Gespräch* is never the one we wanted to conduct but rather one we fall into as it develops. To be in a conversation means allowing oneself to be conducted by the subject matter because a conversation does not have a goal. This is why we cannot decide to become involved in a conversation, assume a position of leadership within it, or become indifferent toward the other in the relationship. Instead, we wait for these features to appear on their own; we are always led by the conversation. However, our being always led by the *Gespräch* does not mean that truth will never appear but rather that it will always be a contingent effect of its own unprogrammed factors, which we never have under control. This is why *Gespräch* is closer to what in English we call "conversation" and not "dialogue," which is a specialized category of conversation aimed at finding truth, as in the Platonic dialogues.

Although Plato probably thought his dialogues were in the slaves' best interest, the fact that he would also consider it necessary to "drag the slave away by force into the light of the sun" if he was not convinced (through the dialogue) implies that Plato was guided by truth. This is why in most of Plato's dialogues truth is not an outcome but is always presupposed by those who opportunely interrogate the others. After all, even though the slave in Plato's *Meno* might discover the geometric truth, he will not have understood it until he also submits to the philosopher's truth. James Risser points out that "most conversations in the dialogues of Plato are not ideal conversations where thinking would be devoted purely to the subject matter talked about. This situation of an impure conversation raises the question for Gadamer as to what constitutes a shared understanding and a real being-with-one-another in conversation."⁸⁰

Despite the fact that all conversations are always directed toward specific agreements, it is important to note that Gadamer is referring to an "agreement" not about truth or content but rather about the maintenance of a common language in an endless conversation. This is why philosophizing "does not just start from zero but rather has to think further and speak further the language we speak."⁸¹ The point is not that everything is language but merely that "Being that can be understood, insofar as it can be understood, is language" because what cannot be understood poses an endless task of finding the right word. This is why in an illuminating interview with Grondin, Gadamer emphasized that

> I have never thought and never ever said that everything is language. Being that can be understood, insofar as it can be understood, is language. This contains a limitation. What cannot be understood can pose an endless task of at least finding a word that comes a little closer to the matter at issue [*die Sache*].⁸²

Heidegger's destruction of metaphysics, whose question about the "whatness of beings" obscured the question of the "thereness of Being," led Gadamer to go further to consider the notion of conversation as the most adequate mode of Being on the way to language. The transformation that takes place in a conversation among speakers allows hermeneutics to leave behind the metaphysical subjectivity of the transcendental ego as well as the meaning-directed intention of the speaker. In sum, if the "conversation" is all we have left, then we can conclude from Gadamer's analysis that conversation, Being's remnant, defines itself precisely "in what aims at being said beyond all words sought after or found" because "in a conversation, it is *something*, that comes to language, not one or the other speaker."[83]

Although it is not explicit whether Gadamer meant conversation or dialogue by *Gespräch*, the fact that truth was significant for him allows us to distinguish his hermeneutics not only from Heidegger's "different conceptual platform" but also from Rorty and Vattimo's weak thought. Also, and most importantly, elucidating this difference allows us to notice how "conversation" is weak in comparison to "dialogue," where truth is the primary goal and control the necessary condition. However, it is just this weakness that responds not only to the "worn-out" condition of Being after its destruction but also to the new postmetaphysical question, "How is it going with Being?" As in a conversation, Being is not set apart but simply interpreted in order to allow us to come to terms with metaphysics, which we cannot overcome but must maintain in order to avoid falling into it.

This hermeneutic conversation is free from any metaphysics, epistemology, or representationalist modalities, and this is why Rorty emphasizes it as the "ultimate context within which knowledge is to be understood."[84] It should not come as a surprise that Rorty's contribution to a collection of essays on the analytic and continental divide in 2003 was entitled "Analytic and Conversational Philosophy" or that one of Vattimo's books is *Farewell to Truth* (2009). Both are invitations not only to enlarge the branches of contemporary philosophy through conversation but also, as Heidegger said, to "remain in conversation with that to which the tradition of philosophy delivers us, that is, liberates us": the Being of beings.

BEING AND TRUTH

Suggesting that Being, after the destruction of metaphysics, ought to be understood as "conversation" is not meant to be a "truer" interpretation of Being than any other but rather to recall how

Being is always at large, that is, unconstrained by truth. The fact that we are led by the conversation instead of leaders of it does not point toward the origin or essence of truth but rather its absence. This, after all, is the meaning of Rorty and Vattimo's titles mention above. In the "conversational philosophy" Rorty calls for, "truth" is absent because, as Vattimo explains, the "relation of thought to the truth of Being, to the original aperture of truth, to the milieu into which Dasein is thrown, is in no sense a cognizance, a theoretical acquisition," but rather "a message that we have to knowingly interpret and transform."[85] In this interpretation, truth does not function anymore as a datum to be known objectively or a norm to be applied once for all but rather as the possibility that the conversation will continue.

While phenomenology, critical theory, and analytic philosophy continue to examine the origin or essence of truth, philosophical hermeneutics has finally begun to emphasize not only why truth is absent but also how philosophy can disregard it in favour of Being. This is possible not only because Being has priority over truth but also because there is no truer interpretation of Being which could justify it. Such a truer interpretation (or "description of Being") would frame philosophy within metaphysics, that is, submit it to realism, science, or a culturally dominant philosophical position. The fact that the history of philosophy is actually constituted by precisely these periodic dominating positions does not justify the search for truth; rather, it calls for different interpretations or events of truth, hence, truth's absence. In sum, from a philosophical position advocating the interpretative nature of truth, hermeneutics has become an ontological account of the remains of Being where truth ceases to have any normative power.

The goal of this section is to outline why the remains of Being are the result of Heidegger's resistance to phenomenology's concept of truth and its metaphysical indifference. This resistance, which is linked to his destruction of metaphysics, allowed hermeneutics to become not only a philosophical position, through Luigi Pareyson, John Sallis, and Georgia Warnke but, moreover, a thought beyond any position, as Rorty and Vattimo have highlighted. Contrary to the majority of hermeneutic philosophers, who believe Heidegger has only "elevated hermeneutics to the centre of philosophical concern,"[86] he is also responsible for disclosing its intrinsic resistance to truth. Although most interpreters agree that Heidegger resisted Husserl's concept of truth, not all hermeneutic philosophers explicitly recognize *resistance* as one of the fundamental characteristics of hermeneutics because of the normative power truth continues to have. As I will explain in chapter 2, this resistance belongs to the anarchic vein of hermeneutics, which is clearly palpable in classic writings by Martin Luther, Sigmund Freud, and Thomas Kuhn. The fact that each of these thinkers highlighted, through different approaches, the inevitable interpretative nature of truth implies the existence of the anarchic strain of hermeneutics, if not its centrality to the system.

The fact that Heidegger elevated the discipline to the centre of ontology and at the same time resisted Husserl's phenomenology through hermeneutics inevitably questions both the concern for truth in philosophical hermeneutics and also the role of interpretation for Heidegger's early formation. After all, his reevaluation of interpretation before *Being and Time* demands that hermeneutics rise above its traditional position as a subordinate discipline of the human sciences to become the self-interpretation of the human and social sciences. As the publication of Heidegger's early courses indicates, hermeneutics, like Christianity, has not only been constantly present throughout the formation of Western human sciences but also determinate in the reception of phenomenology. This is probably why Theodore Kisiel, in his classic study on the genesis of *Being and Time*, emphasized that the origin of this text lies "in the first analysis of the environing world within the context of a 'hermeneutics of facticity.'"[87] Such facticity does not allude to different relations with the world, ourselves, or others but rather to the totality of these relations, that is, the ontological relation. Even before the publication of *Being and Time* Heidegger already indicated that "truth" is not

> a relation that is "just there" between two beings that themselves are "just there" – one mental, the other physical. Nor is it a coordination, as philosophers like to say these days. If

it is a relation at all, it is one that has no analogies with any other relation between beings. If I may put it this way, it is the relation of existence as such to its very world. It is the world-openness of existence that is itself uncovered – existence whose very being unto the world gets disclosed/uncovered in and with its being unto the world.[88]

Before venturing into the concept of truth it is important to understand why the collaboration between Heidegger and Husserl came to an end. The break between the two philosophers has been at the centre of a great number of studies that sought either to demonstrate how the disciple distanced himself from the teacher or to show how much Heidegger was dependent on phenomenology. While both interpretations are vital to understand contemporary philosophy, it is also important to stress why Heidegger distanced himself from a philosophical position that was at the peak of its success. Heidegger was already dissociating from Husserl's concept of truth, as the passage just quoted shows, but the collaboration broke off when the two worked together on the article "Phenomenology" for the fourteenth edition of the *Encyclopedia Britannica* (1929). Heidegger ended the collaboration because Husserl not only continued to interpret phenomenology metaphysically but also attempted to dissolve philosophy in a series of regional ontologies. For Heidegger this dissolution represented the attempt to develop the metaphysical dream that he was trying to overcome. Although he did not refer explicitly to hermeneutics as an alternative to phenomenology, the latter did not seem to him appropriate for overcoming metaphysics and its concept of truth, in other words, for operating beyond metaphysical frames.

These frames, common also to other philosophical positions, are founded upon the fundamental question of ontology, "Why are there beings at all instead of nothing?" This formulation is not only at the core of Western ontology but also the expression of a fundamental duplicity in Being that articulates its presence by splitting, that is, by duplicating Being. As Tugendhat explained, in such duplicity "Being is" only as long as the two parts are joined, creating a relation between two terms where one refers to the other as the predicate and subject. The coupling of "subject" and "predicate" is not only a simple logical or verbal structure but the description of this duplication, in which both parts are connected.⁸⁹ This connection is also present in the correspondence theory of truth. As Ernst Tugendhat recalls, already in the

> Middle Ages a definition came into fashion according to which truth was supposed to consist in the correspondence of thought with the thing, *adaequatio intellectus et rei*. This formulation can be understood to contain a correct though preliminary definition of the word true; but it can just as easily be interpreted in a way that results in nonsense. It is only meaningful (1) if both sides are understood propositionally, and (2) if the side of thinking is also interpreted objectively in the sense of what is thought, believed, or asserted.⁹⁰

Tugendhat is among Heidegger's most important critics not only because he studied under Heidegger in Freiburg but also because he pointed out that by resisting Husserl's phenomenology Heidegger also "lost" the concept of truth through hermeneutics. This was an error he should have avoided and one that undermined his fundamental ontology as well his politics because philosophy's goal is "to organize the whole of human life around truth, in other words, around the idea of a life conducted with critical responsibility."⁹¹ This is why in his classic study on Husserl's and Heidegger's concepts of truth, Tugendhat points out how the specific Husserlian sense of truth in terms of a difference between mere "intention" and the matter "itself" also presupposes the duplicity of Being common to this medieval metaphysical tradition as it distinguishes between the manner in which something in fact appears and the manner in which it "itself" is. Having said this, a proposition, for example, will be true only if it refers to things in a way that permits them to be seen as they are in themselves. This is why the truth of statements is also grounded in a metaphysical, preliminary aesthetic structure: the truth of intuition.

In order to resist Husserl's progression within traditional logics, Heidegger substituted interpretation, which presents an alternative and preliminary structure of the statement, for this aesthetic intuition. But if the statement (the "apophantic as") must be grounded in interpretation (the "hermeneutic as"), it is not because the latter is *truer* than the former but because the statement's truth is actually rooted in the disclosedness of Dasein's understanding, which determines not only prelinguistic duplicity but also its adequacy and correspondence. This is why Heidegger, in *Being and Time*, specified that

> the statement is not the primary "locus" of truth but the *other way around*: the statement as a mode of appropriation of discoveredness and as a way of being-in-the-world is based in discovering, or in the *disclosedness* of Dasein. The most primordial "truth" is the "locus" of the statement and the ontological condition of the possibility that statement can be true or false (discovering or covering over).[92]

Heidegger, by separating evidence from the adequation formula and correspondence from the appearance formula, proposed a concept of truth that consists of the self-manifestation of Being in its unconcealment. But, as Tugendhat pointed out, truth as uncovering (*Unverborgenheit*) or disclosure (*Erschlossenheit*) does not have anything to do with sentences that declare something because it consists only in the "event" of this same unconcealment. According to Tugendhat and many other philosophers, such as Karl-Otto Apel and Jürgen Habermas,[93] even if Heidegger retained the word truth, it still "lost" its specific meaning since it is transposed "without further justification to all disclosedness of entities within-the-world,"[94] that is, both true and false statements. A confirmation of this can also be found in Heidegger who, according to Apel,[95] after learning of Tugendhat's observations, decided to clarify the matter:

> To raise the question of *aletheia*, of unconcealment as such, is not the same as raising the question of truth. For this reason, it was inadequate and misleading to call *aletheia* in the sense of opening, truth ... How the attempt to think a matter can

at times stray from that which a decisive insight has already shown, is demonstrated by a passage from *Being and Time* (1927). To translate this word (*aletheia*) as "truth," and, above all, to define this expression conceptually in theoretical ways, is to cover up the meaning of what the Greeks made "self-evidently" basic for the terminological use of *aletheia* as a prephilosophical way of understanding it.[96]

Whether or not this was a "self-correction," as Apel would like to believe, it confirms that Heidegger was not looking for a mere concept of truth or a concept of truth to distinguish true from false, un-valid from valid, good from evil, but a "different conceptual platform" as Pöggeler pointed out. This platform does not represent a progression toward truth but rather an alternative between "truth" and "truth's absence" or between knowledge and thought. This alternative does not imply that "the 'correspondence theory of truth' is wrong but only superficial."[97] After all, disclosedness, as John Sallis explained, "is a matter neither *of* intuition nor *for* intuition. The originary phenomenon of truth, truth as disclosedness, is a truth that is not of knowledge."[98]

In sum, while knowledge belongs within a paradigm in which truth and error operate, thought is the realm where truth, error, and paradigms occur. Although such occurrence (also called "event" by Heidegger) may be interpreted as truth, it actually indicates truth's absence, given it is not something "outside" or "above" us but rather something that belongs to us: "Truth," Heidegger states, "makes it ontologically possible that we can be in such a way that we presuppose something." This is why "Being – not entities – is something which 'there is' ['*gibt es*'] only in so far [*solange*] as truth is. Beings are discovered only when Dasein is, and only as long as Dasein is are they disclosed."[99] What Heidegger is trying to say, as Vattimo put it, is that "there is Being, not beings, if there is truth. There is Being to the extent that there are not just, or not primarily, beings."[100] But if the event of disclosure is not useful to distinguish between Being and beings, true and false, or good or evil actions, what is it philosophically productive for? Why is it necessary? The answer to this question lies in *freedom*, that is, in the possibility of Being at large. For Heidegger,

> freedom is not merely what common sense is content to let pass under this name: the caprice, turning up occasionally in our choosing, of inclining in this or that direction. Freedom is not mere absence of constraint with respect to what we can or cannot do. Nor is it on the other hand mere readiness for what is required and necessary (and so somehow a being). Prior to all this ("negative" and "positive" freedom), freedom is engagement in the disclosure of beings as such. Disclosedness itself is conserved in ek-sistent engagement, through which the openness of the open region, i.e., the "there" ["*Da*"], is that it is.[101]

So freedom, similar to truth as disclosedness, is prior to any property of the subject or intersubjective activity: it is a mode of Being-in-the-world. Although it is only after *Being and Time* that Heidegger refers to freedom as existential, that is, as one of the fundamental conditions of world-disclosure, it became central to his ontology as it prefigures human subjectivity. "The essence of truth reveals itself as freedom" because it is "the ground of the possibility of Dasein."[102] Nichols Robert explains that Heidegger's "understanding of freedom is taken up increasingly as a mode or style of existence, rather than as a property of the subject or a strategic form of action outside of or in resistance to power." Heidegger argues that the essence of truth is freedom, the freedom to let beings emerge, unveil, and be.

If philosophy, as Heidegger demanded, "must at all times work out Being for itself anew," then truth must allow Being to take place, facilitate its occurrence, and let it be. This is why Heidegger's new fundamental question of philosophy – "How is it going with Being?" – was meant not only to maintain unconcealed the horizon for further Being but also to resist the relation or coordination of beings, that is, truth as correspondence. Contrary to the traditional metaphysical question, where truth was sought in a correspondence between beings and Being, in this new question the priority is given to the possibility of "working out" Being again, that is, generating further Being even though it has become the "fading last echo of a mere hollow word."¹⁰³ And so truth as disclosedness, instead of a contribution to the relation between beings, underlines the resistance to this same relation, which is responsible not only for forgetting Being but also for submitting parts of contemporary philosophy to realism. Given that it is only within truth's absence that Being takes place, ontology can no longer refer to Being's presence (which frames it within truth) but must rather rely on its own existential Being. This is why, as Brice Wachterhauser said, what Heidegger's disclosedness

> points to is the privileged place that human being has in the economy of Being. Human beings are capable of truth because they find themselves in the clearing (*Lichtung*) of Being's disclosure, i.e., they stand in reality and open to reality in the sense of that they experience reality as accessible to understanding, as showing itself to us in ways that are fundamentally trustworthy both epistemically and practically.¹⁰⁴

But how does such Being relate to metaphysics? If metaphysics could be overcome once for all (*Überwindung*) freedom would imply a correspondence, that is, a truth we would have to submit to. This submission is evident in the "indifference" Heidegger relates to the metaphysical oblivion of Being in *Mindfulness*. In this important treatise of 1938–39 the German thinker points out how this forgetfulness is not "even an error – only a matter of indifference"¹⁰⁵ tied to the aesthetic intuition of phenomenology. The difference between "error" and "indifference" is essential to understanding the emergence of Being's remnants after the deconstruction of metaphysics. While an error could be corrected, if acknowledged as such, indifference discards what is not significant whether it is correct or erroneous. The fact that metaphysics can only be overcome through a productive twisting, that is, *Verwindung* and not *Überwindung*, implies an actual resistance to this indifference, which, as I claimed at the outset, is constitutive of hermeneutics. Ontology, after metaphysics, instead of relying on presences must rely on its own resistance to presences or, which is the same, the remains of Being.

If a response to the new fundamental question of philosophy ("How is it going with Being?") is possible within the remains of Being, it is not because of philosophy's accuracy but rather its lack of accuracy, that is, "truth's absence." These remains are the result of Heidegger's destruction of metaphysics where Being – instead of another presence in accordance with an empirical image or ideal – becomes the absence, discharge, or weakness of that truth claim. This absence encompasses everything that does not work, that is, that does not function through such an accordance with truth, especially those philosophical positions constantly accused of relativism, irrationalism, and nihilism, such as pragmatism, critical theory, and hermeneutics. These features, which could be grouped under the general rubric of "weak thought," are hermeneutic ontology's means of maintaining not only the conflict of interpretation and the resistance to metaphysics but also the generation of Being, which is possible only as long truth is absent. But just as truth as correspondence is possible only within disclosure, so is Being possible only within the remains of Being. As Derrida explains:

> The remainder *is* not, it is not a Being, not a modification of that which is. Like the trace, the remaining offers itself for thought before or beyond Being. It is inaccessible to a straightforward intuitive perception (since it refers to something wholly other, it inscribes in itself something of the infinitely other), and it escapes all forms of prehension, all forms of monumentalization, and all forms of archivation. Often, like the trace, I associate it with ashes: remains without a substantial remainder, essentially, but which have to be taken account of and without which there would be neither accounting nor calculation, nor a principle of reason able to give an account or a rationale (*reddere rationem*), nor a Being as such. That is why there are *remainder effects*, in the sense of a result or a present, idealizable, ideally iterable residue.[106]

Being and Truth

If truth is absent in the "trace," "event," "conversation," and other weak concepts, it is not because they are not true or cannot be defined but rather because they belong to the remains of Being, that is, where not "what is" but what "remains" is relevant for philosophy. Remnants are those concepts that by resisting truth accordance and its inevitable realism not only escape "all forms of prehension, monumentalization, and archivation" but also "exist" since, as Jean-Luc Nancy stated, only "what remains thus, or what is *coming* and does not stop coming as what remains, is what we call *existence*."[107]

Dasein's existence takes place in the same way as the truth of the trace, event, and conversation, that is, as "what is coming," as the resistance to the "present" of "presence." Just as we are not in control of the outcome of these remnants, neither are we in control of "what is coming," that is, of the future. Here Heidegger's difference between the past as "*vergangen*" and as "*gewesen*" is vital. While in the former the past becomes an irrevocable necessity we must submit to, in the later it means accepting history as open to the future, as a having-been that still offers the possibility of freely deciding our lives without being encapsulated in a true knowledge. As we can see, truth's absence becomes the resistance to existence's frame or to a state of Being where history is reduced to the present.

Heidegger's stressing the "futural" possibility of hermeneutics as its first principle does not favour the conservative nature of the tradition, as Gadamer or Ricoeur would have it, but rather "what is coming," that is, the possibility of different disclosures and interpretations. Although different interpretations demand the absence of truth in order to take place, such absence also includes the possibility of freedom, which is what differentiates Dasein from beings. This is why if Dasein does not want to be reduced to another present being but instead exist, it must engage in hermeneutic ontology and the conflict of interpretations, which, instead of justifications for descriptions, seeks disclosures for further Being. Such disclosures belong to the remains of Being, where, as Schürmann said, "much remains for us to think but little for us to know."[108]

In sum, Being at large is possible only in the absence of truth, that is, of metaphysical correspondence. Freedom takes place as an engagement in disclosures that are not meant for knowledge but rather to think against the indifference that embraces metaphysics. This indifference is absent in the remains of Being because they emerge precisely to resist metaphysical framing and the imposition of truth claims on Being and beings.

Part Two

INTERPRETATION

In the end, hermeneutic thinkers are more or less explicitly accused of being crypto-terrorists and fomenters of social disorder. Confronted by the tightening of the social order that accompanies globalization, hermeneutics becomes aware of its own nihilistic vocation; and it takes note of the menace that every pretense of absolute truth represents for freedom and thus for the history of Being.

– Gianni Vattimo, *Being and Its Surroundings*

In the second half of the twentieth century, interpretation became a *koiné* – a common language through which philosophical thought spread everywhere. This could not have happened without Hans-Georg Gadamer. He is considered not only Martin Heidegger's most distinguished disciple but also the architect of modern hermeneutics. His magnum opus of 1960 first articulated a conception of hermeneutics in its universality and enabled its expansion into the wider framework of contemporary philosophical debate. Although Gadamer was appalled by his teacher's political views and choices, he was also accused in 1971 by Jürgen Habermas and his followers from the 1968 German student revolt of being too conservative. This accusation was based on his closeness with Heidegger and on the uncritical acceptance of tradition in his hermeneutics, which his critics believed restricted its ability for radical critical reflection. While it was certainly true that Gadamer was no radical, the acceptance of tradition imputed to hermeneutics is inseparable from its role in criticizing existing practices. It turns out that hermeneutics is more a "critical theory" than the thought of the members of the Frankfurt School, who established their critical functions on metaphysical ideals, such as Habermas's communicative or Karl-Otto Apel's transcendental conditions of rationality. Nonetheless, these accusations led to a common view of hermeneutics as a conservative philosophical position, which indirectly contributed to a general tendency to overlook an essential feature of interpretation: its anarchic vein.

The goal of this chapter is to outline the anarchic vein that runs through the work of six important hermeneutic thinkers and free interpretation of their ideas from the conservative approach that still characterizes most introductions to and histories of hermeneutics. This approach has led to the exclusion of some radical figures, such as Friedrich Nietzsche, and has limited the presentation of hermeneutics as a philosophical school with a unified history.[1] An inability or refusal to individuate the philosophical import of interpretation beyond its traditional role (as a technique for ensuring a correct understanding of texts from jurisprudence, theology, or philology) is certainly at the origin of these restrictions. Gadamer is not solely responsible for this limitation of the horizon of hermeneutics, but his acceptance of tradition and fusion of fields for the sake of dialogue has induced many of his followers to set aside the philosophy's anarchic vein when reconstructing its history. At most, hermeneutics has been presented as a radical theory of the interpretative character of every experience of truth, but always for the peaceful, innocent, and conciliatory purpose of dialogue. But as Gianni Vattimo said, hermeneutics "can no longer be presented, if it was ever able to be, as an innocent theory of the interpretative character of every experience of truth" because there is much more at stake.[2]

Contemporary thought has inherited from Gadamer a philosophical stance that is continuously overcoming itself, whose applications and consequences he could not have foreseen. While some interpreters consider the recent feminist, political, and environmental developments on hermeneutics to be foreign to Gadamer's philosophical project, others find that they are connected to his thought.³ There are signs in his writings that he predicted and possibly wished to see these developments. One of these is his definition of the classics. As he pointed out in *Truth and Method* it's not the source or origin that makes a classic but rather its effects and consequences, that is, those uncontrollable features that also constitute its essence.⁴ For those who consider the effects and consequences of hermeneutics, such as a canon of classics, more significant than its origin, inheriting Gadamer's philosophy of interpretation does not mean accepting the discipline's origins and history as essence but rather continue to interpret them. Interpretation, as Jeff Malpas explains, never comes "to an end – or, at least, any ending to which interpretation comes is always temporary, always contingent, always open to revision. As hermeneutics is hermeneutical, so such indeterminacy applies to hermeneutics itself."⁵

This indeterminacy is manifest in the different interpretations that have been given to Gadamer's own history of hermeneutics and that reveal how its origins cannot be established once and for all but must always be sought through diverse interpretations. While some histories situate the creation of philosophical hermeneutics in Aristotle's treatise *Peri hermeneias* (*De interpretatione*), others proclaim that it was formed two millennia later by Flacius, in *Clavis scripturae sacrae*, or even later, in the seventeenth century, when Johann Dannhauer introduced for the first time the Latin word *hermeneutica* as a necessary requirement for those sciences that relied on the interpretation of texts. Also theological hermeneutics (*hermeneutica sacra*) and juridical hermeneutics (*hermeneutica juris*) play different roles: the former continues to condition the connection of hermeneutics and religion (in the work of John D. Caputo and Richard Kearney) and the latter is an indication of interpretation's critical role in society (in the work of Georgia Warnke and Stanley Rosen). Heidegger, who presented a history of hermeneutics in 1923 before Gadamer's, went as far as to criticize the different hermeneutics that emerged after the seventeenth century because the discipline's "performance sense" and "practical dimension" were transformed into "method," "doctrine," and "discipline." Saint Augustine, for Heidegger, provides the first "'hermeneutics' in grand style."⁶

Although Gadamer was primarily interested in stressing how art, like science, also manifests truth claims, he was also concerned for the fate of hermeneutics within the academy. This led him to maintain the classical distinction between *Geisteswissenschaften*, the "human" or "moral" sciences, and *Naturwissenschaften*, the natural sciences. While this distinction has permitted hermeneutics to rely upon tradition, defend the extra-methodological truth of the human sciences, and protect the discipline within the academy, it has also concealed its anarchic vein. But as practised by the "ancients and their humanist admirers," as Kathy Eden points out, "interpretation is by and large adversarial, an antagonistic affair."[7] Thus, what "counts as belonging to the hermeneutic 'tradition,' and how the history of hermeneutics should be configured, is thus itself a hermeneutic problem."[8] This configuration led Vattimo to suggest that "the history of modern hermeneutics, and, so far as we can imagine, also its future, is a history of 'excess' – of the transgression of limits, or, to use another idiom, the history of a continuous 'overflowing.'"[9] And Gerald L. Bruns stresses how

> hermeneutics is a loose and baggy monster, or anyhow a less than fully disciplined body of thinking, whose inventory of topics spreads out over many different historical, cultural, and intellectual contexts. Hermeneutics is "anarchic" in Rainer Schürmann's sense of this word; it does not try to assault its *Sache* but rather tries to grant what is singular and unrepeatable an open field.[10]

Eden, Vattimo, and Bruns raise doubts about whether there is such a thing as an origin, a history, or any unified development of hermeneutics, but they also acknowledge the discipline's anarchic vein. This vein is etymologically evident in the god Hermes, "the many-sided, uncontainable, nocturnal transgressor,"[11] whose role is central in both in the etymological and historical development of hermeneutics.

The very term "hermeneutics" comes from a family of Ancient Greek terms: *hermeneuein* or *hermêneusai* and *hermêneia* to designate an activity, *hermênês* to designate the individual who carries out this activity, and *hermêneutikê* to designate a particular discipline associated with this activity. Given this ancient provenance of the word, it would seem not only that it makes sense to speak of an "Ancient Hermeneutics," but that hermeneutics is something distinctively characteristic of Ancient Greek thought.¹²

This individual, as Francisco Gonzalez clarifies, is the messenger god Hermes, whose name points back to his winged feet. He was renowned for his speed, athleticism, and swiftness as he exercised the practical activity of delivering the announcements, warnings, and prophecies of the gods of Olympus. In the *Cratylus* (407e), *Ion* (534e), and *Symposium* (202e), Plato connects the term *hermênea* etymologically to the name of the god Hermes and presents hermeneutics both as a theory of reception and "as a practice for transmission and mediation": Hermes must transmit what is beyond human understanding in a form that human intelligence can grasp. Nonetheless, in this transmission, Hermes was often accused of treachery, thievery, and even anarchy because the messages were never accurate; in other words, his interpretations always altered the original meanings. This is why, as Jean Greisch explains, "Hermes is not only the messenger of the divine; he is also the god of travelers, diplomats, and outlaws."¹³

Hermes' alterations are the real contribution of interpretation; unlike description, which pursues the ideal of total explanation, interpretation adds new vitality. This vitality is manifest in many hermeneutic thinkers: Dilthey (who in the seventeenth century was the first to systematically trace the history of hermeneutics) saw in the vitalist essence of hermeneutics the priority of interpretation over theoretical criticism, scientific inquiry, and literary construction. Friedrich Schleiermacher believed it could help us understand a work "at first just as well and then better than its author."¹⁴ And Nietzsche recognized that "facts is precisely what there is not, only interpretations … is it necessary to posit an interpreter behind the interpretation? Even this is invention, hypothesis."¹⁵ In sum, if, as Gadamer says, "interpretation is an insertion [*Einlegen*] of meaning and not a discovery [*Finden*] of it,"¹⁶ then the hermeneuticist, according to Vattimo "must also become, fatally, a militant – the question is: for which cause?"¹⁷

As we can see, hermeneutics in the twenty-first century cannot be reduced to a philosophical discipline such as aesthetics nor to a philosophical school such as positivism. There is more at stake in the process of interpretation, which transcends disciplinary parameters and school ambitions. The world of hermeneutics is not an "object" that can be observed from different points of view and that offers various interpretations. It is a thought-world in continuous movement. If this world does not reveal itself to the perceptions of human beings as a continuous narrative, it's not simply because this is an age of alternative facts. Rather, this reticence emerges because we are not passive describers. As engaged performers we must always strive – through interpretation – for freedom. This is why the revolutionary role that interpretation had in major social political events (Richard Rorty's departure from analytic philosophy, Freud's psychoanalytic approach, or Luther's translation of the Bible) did not emerge from its dialogical ambitions but rather from its anarchic vein. Anarchy, as Reiner Schürmann said, is not something opposed to "rules," "regulations," and "methods" but to the universal "rule," "regulation," and "method" that obstruct our existence, that is, our freedom.¹⁸ In line with Schürmann's definition, Simon Critchley specifies that

> anarchism is not so much a grand unified theory of revolution based on a socio-economic metaphysics and a philosophy of history, as a moral conviction, an ethical disposition that finds expression in practice and as practice. Anarchism is a different way of conceiving and enacting social relations between people, where they are not defined by the authority of the state, the law and the police, but by free agreement between them.¹⁹

Given the impracticality of outlining the anarchic vein that runs through the full history of hermeneutics, this chapter will have to leave out many important figures, such as Origen, Georg

Friedrich Meier, and Luigi Pareyson. Instead, it will interpret the works of six thinkers in inverse order, that is, moving back from the twenty-first century to the patristic period. This method is intrinsically related to the ontological transformation hermeneutics underwent with Heidegger. This transformation elevated interpretation to the centre of philosophical discussion (Emilio Betti, Eric D. Hirsch, and others systematize it as an academic discipline among others) and also stresses the fundamental relation between existence and interpretation. If, as Heidegger insisted, this is not a simple relation between two beings but primarily an ontological relation, then the history of hermeneutics can be read as the history of an existential struggle for our own freedom.

In this struggle, Being, rather than an object, becomes our own interpretation as thrown projects, that is, an active involvement against external impositions. The history of this struggle does not belong to the powerful, those "winners" whose history is always presented as continuous and rational but rather, as Walter Benjamin pointed out, to the "oppressed" whose past seems "discontinuous" and "erroneous" and is therefore often forgotten. It is patently inaccurate to think of Rorty, Freud, and Luther as unrecognized thinkers, but their use of interpretation, as we will see, took the form of resistance, transgression, and alteration in order to allow a freer existence. In this condition hermeneutics not only allows but welcomes an inverse presentation because, contrary to the commonly accepted historiography (that presents a conservative development of hermeneutics), a revelation of the anarchic vein in hermeneutics must stress the effort that interpretation always demands from us.

While some might interpret this historical approach as a simple postmodern variation of Hayden White's rejection of causality in history or Michel Foucault's genealogic counter-history, its aim is not to highlight the arbitrariness of common chronological reconstructions in order to debate the meaning of history but to find a method that can expose the anarchic vein of hermeneutics. A simple chronological reconstruction would risk presenting hermeneutics as a controllable discipline and its practitioners as obedient disciples who will submit to an irrevocable past regardless of their interpretations. Instead, given the ontological relation between interpretation and existence, history becomes the opportunity to interpret and project our existence in new ways. The resistances (in Vattimo and Rorty), transgressions (in Freud and Nietzsche), and alterations (in Luther and Augustine) this chapter outlines will show how an existential effort is always required in interpretation to achieve free existence.

INTERPRETATION AND RESISTANCE

Many contemporary histories, introductions, and companions to hermeneutics pair the philosophers Gianni Vattimo and Richard Rorty. A recent example is John D. Caputo's *Hermeneutics: Facts and Interpretation in the Age of Information* (2018), where both authors as introduced as "positively roguish figures who enjoyed playing the role of Hermes the prankster to their respective Apollos."[20] Vattimo and Rorty have played this role with Gadamer's hermeneutics through attributing a different meaning to dialogue, preferring the weaker term "conversation," and, most of all, they stress the emancipatory role they believe hermeneutics can play in our lives.

Although interpretation plays a different role in their resistances – Vattimo against the political consequences of globalization and Rorty against the rigidity of analytic philosophy – the anarchic vein of hermeneutics is clear in their work as they both strive for political and cultural freedom. This vein, in line with Schürmann and Critchley's definition of anarchy mentioned above, is not the product of a grand and unified theory but rather of ethical disposition, practices, and rules. The ethical effort follows from interpretation's demand that we take a stance, that is, that we choose sides whenever possible. Vattimo's and Rorty's decision to take their own stances was not without consequences for their careers. After his political tenure in the European Union, Vattimo was unable to proceed in Italian national politics. And Rorty had to move to comparative literature departments since he was regarded as a traitor by most of his colleagues in philosophy departments. The goal of this section is to understand how the anarchic vein of hermeneutics has drawn these thinkers to resist in such important matters.[21]

Vattimo indicates that the emphasis on religion and politics one often sees in contemporary hermeneutics is not only a development of Gadamer's extramethodical experience of truth but also a response to our existential condition in the twenty-first century. This condition has always been at the centre of his investigations, the main concern of which is to weaken the strong and violent structures of metaphysics through interpretation. His philosophical goal, as Robert Valgenti points out, "is to bring a certain hermeneutic insight into the events of our current age, to interpret the voices that are often ignored in the name of political, religious, and economic 'truths,' and to empower those who seek to express themselves in a world capable of understanding but often hostile to it."[22] This explains Vattimo's intellectual trajectory: after proposing a nihilist interpretation of Heidegger through Nietzsche in the 1980s and weakening the fundamentalist traits of religion in the 1990s, in the last decades the Italian thinker has turned to the techno-scientific transformation that politics has undergone in the West.

Vattimo draws on Heidegger's notion of *Gestell* (which can also be translated as framework or enframing) and *Notlosigkeit* (often rendered as lack or absence) to outline the essence of democracies today. He uses the first term to indicate the culmination of metaphysics, that is, the reduction of beings to what is calculable and manipulable by science. Vattimo makes use of the second to reveal the current political condition, where the "greatest emergency is the absence of emergency." These concepts explain the increasing homologization of the political, economic, and social structures of power that have now framed democracies in the service of the laws of neoliberal capitalism. The problem today is not only that neoliberalism has succeeded but, most of all, *how* it has removed freedom from democracy, evident in the absence of opposition parties in recent technical and bipartisan governments across Europe.

According to Vattimo, the European Union, which represents the incarnation of these technical governments, has relied too much on those "technicians" whose only responsibility is to assure the "functioning of the globalized machine." These technicians have refinanced banks, reduced welfare, and also intensified the strictures of social order after 9/11. Vattimo calls this intensification, which has now gained further strength with the rise of right-wing populist politicians throughout the world, a "retour a l'ordre," a return to order that is required by the logic of globalization. The problem of contemporary democracies, framed by metaphysics, is that they are determined by the triumph of technology, in which scientific ideal of objectivity becomes an instrument of policing, oppression, and control.

> Here "policing" takes many different forms: the "policing" of thought (notably the proponents of analytic epistemology), the "policing" of the leading classes (consider the "neo-realism" of the major academic journals, as well as of the international "mainstream" media), the "policing" of governments (in the form, for instance, of cultural policies "compliant with the current order," "neutral" audit and assurance exercises and processes, or "objective" evaluation of scientific productivity – the latter, starting from the privilege of English, represent a continuation of old imperialist and colonialist policies by other means).[23]

Vattimo is convinced that globalization represents a more advanced and established phase of Adorno and Horkheimer's "die totale Verwaltung," the total administrative/organizational system where rationality is turned into generalized oppression. This oppression is evident in the ongoing devastation of regional communities and cultures in the service of manufacture and commerce and in the continued degradation of the environment as the systems of technological control refuse to surrender any profit in order to combat climate change. This is why even in those economically central parts of the world where globalization has not yet produced the obvious disastrous effects that are visible in the peripheries, one feels the existential and, with that, material intolerability of globalization. This nightmare condition grew out of the philosophical and political "realist" position that considers technology and science to be "neutral," when, in fact, scientists and scientific research are also conditioned through the funds and policies of foundations and governments, which instil in those grants their imperial ambitions.

These ambitions are particularly evident in the unexpected connection between the ideology of George W. Bush and the philosophical realism of John Searle. Searle insists that philosophy must submit to scientific principles, that the findings of research must condition the explorations of thought. This philosophy finds practical expression in an ideology that justified invasion and war on resolutions that are calculable and manipulable only by hard sciences. According to Vattimo, "The Searle–Bush ideology wants to purify philosophy from hermeneutic relativism, which appears as a threat to the official, scientific, truth, whose connections to the social and economic power do not need to be proved, if one thinks of the public (military) and private money involved in the modern scientific enterprise."²⁴ It should not come as a surprise that Bush honoured Searle with the National Humanities Medal in 2004 for his "efforts to deepen understanding of the human mind, for using his writings to shape modern thought, defend reason and objectivity and define debate about the nature of artificial intelligence."

Hermeneutics is the best candidate to threaten and unmask this complicity – coercive power and metaphysical scientism – because of its nihilist vocation, Vattimo has been developing through Nietzsche's and Heidegger's writings since the seventies. "But for Vattimo, the advent of nihilism is not to be taken as a negative state. Insofar as it entails the dissolution of foundations and the restraints imposed by the logic of demonstration, it has something of the character of emancipation, where constraints are shed and we gain opportunities to choose."²⁵

In order to resist the return to order, Vattimo recommends understanding interpretation from an ontological, practical, and nihilist point of view, that is, in such a form to hold Being open to different events. These events are necessary to resist the "neutralizing" effects of realist official truth, a resistance necessary not only for the survival of economically marginalized cultures but even for the continuation of life on earth. Life requires that the event of Being be held open because the impositions of authority threatens human life: there is a direct line from subsuming interpretative thought "realist" findings to the loss of breathable air and drinkable water and the possibility of extinction. In this condition, hermeneutics, understood as a philosophy of practice striving for existence, takes the form of a political or, at least, existential commitment, meant to stir and shake those who would obstruct our involvement in the world, that is, the future.

> The world of the future – as seen by hermeneutics, as searched for by hermeneutics – is a world where the "objective" constraints, the "principle of reality" ... must increasingly be challenged by the world of dialogue and conversation, by the world of the truth-event, by the world of a progressive symbolization in which objects move into the background as that which supports the engagement between subjects and in which the violence of immediacy is also thereby reduced.[26]

The significance of hermeneutics for Vattimo does not consist in being argumentatively preferable to other stances or in its ability to justify its neutrality but rather in the intensity of the interpreter's philosophical involvement in the problem at stake. This is why, contrary to philosophers in Searle's vein, who have found in science a way to participate in the general "return to order" required by the logic of globalization and so join the side of the "winners," hermeneutic thinkers must demonstrate that "the claims of truth are always, also, and above all claims to power; and ... that rational human coexistence is possible without 'the truth,' namely with regard to the plurality of values and worldviews that constitute the richness, rather than the danger, of humanity." Vattimo perceives interpretation as a "a virus, a kind of *pharmakon* that infects everything it comes into contact with."[27] And contracting this virus entails the necessity of becoming an "autonomous interpreter"; otherwise, one would no longer live "like a person but like a number, a statistical item in the system of production or consumption."[28]

The fact that hermeneutics does not submit its interpretive freedom to description but rather involves us from the beginning as interpreters – concerned human beings – is an indication of its practical nature. Vattimo explains this practical feature by inverting Marx's famous thesis on Feuerbach about philosophers only interpret the world rather than trying to change it: "Until now, philosophers thought they were only interpreting the world, yet they were truly changing it."²⁹ *To interpret is already to change the world because it always includes a new contribution*. In this way Marx's thesis no longer takes on a metaphysical or positivistic meaning but can be understood "in light of the Heideggerian notion of the event that is always necessarily interpretation and transformation, namely, authentic praxis."³⁰ The transformation of hermeneutics into a philosophy of dangerous praxis does not necessarily mean that it is a philosophy of conflict, but certainly it is not a theory for conciliation on the basis of scientific truth, objectivity, and reality. Knowledge is not the mirror of nature. One can no longer insist that the world is given objectively as a knowable whole; it exists – Being exists – only through events in search of interpretations.

The relation between hermeneutics and nihilism is not based on their common distrust for truth and foundational bases of knowledge and morality but rather on their status as events of history. Nihilism, as eloquently narrated by Nietzsche and taken up again by Heidegger, is the progressive dissolution of theory, that is, a response to the end of metaphysics, and hermeneutics is resistance to the absolutist claims of social, religious, and political power. For Vattimo, nihilism and hermeneutics are forms to defend the event of Being against the imposition of realism and its authority. "Confronted by the tightening of the social order that accompanies globalization, hermeneutics becomes aware of its own nihilistic vocation; and it takes note of the menace that every pretense of absolute truth represents for freedom *and thus for the history of Being*."³¹

While some might consider this ontological, practical, and nihilist disposition of interpretation an exaggeration, Vattimo believes this characterization to be central to the transformation of hermeneutics from a Gadamerian philosophy of dialogue to one of anarchic excess. After all, the intolerance toward anarchic hermeneutics within the academy arises from accusations of exaggeration, which have always marginalized its thinkers:

> Hermeneutics is forbidden from transgressing the proper limits of academic "good manners," limits that are essentially those of "descriptive" metaphysics: there is a thing in front of me, "the world out here," I describe it, I analyze it; I also judge it and condemn it (as absurd, false, morally unacceptable ...); limits that depend always on assuming the validity of the distinction between subject and object – the very distinction which does not hold within the *Geisteswissenschaften*, the human sciences, and whose rejection gives rise to the "excess" of hermeneutics – an excess that has an impact like that of a "terrorist" attack, even if an attack of ideas.[32]

Interpretation for Vattimo is a vital practice, a philosophy of praxis, where Being's event is always held open for existential purposes. But as a vital practice interpretation provides a contrast not only for the passive acceptance that characterizes realist descriptions but also for those limits that Vattimo refers to in the passage above. As David Webb points out, it is important to remember that interpretation's vital activity is an engagement "with its own conditions in such a way that it modifies the form of its own practice; partly in response to the historical situation in which it finds itself, and partly as a contribution to reshaping that situation."[33]

So the anarchic vein of Vattimo's hermeneutics stresses the absence of freedom in framed democracies, technological globalization, and intellectual realism. What is at stake in hermeneutics is a "reformation of the world" that must be "undertaken by a militant hermeneutics with all the tools of the humanities at its disposal – philosophy, theology, fine arts, law, politics."[34]

This reformation is evident in Rorty's resistance to analytic philosophy, which had a shocking impact within American academy – like that of a "terrorist attack" as Vattimo might say

– considering that Rorty was formed within the analytical tradition and was a respectful member of that community. Rorty's efforts to develop a hermeneutic therapeutic alternative to the epistemologically centred analytic philosophy being practised by his mentors and colleagues throughout the United States was meant to reform not only philosophy but also culture in general, which he hoped would become "conversationalist." Although Rorty often seemed dismissive of "the pretensions of his own profession," Martin Woessner is right to stress that he was "nevertheless committed to highlighting its potential contributions to the concrete causes of social justice."[35] This is probably why he spent most of his life, as he said, "looking for a coherent and convincing way of formulating my worries about what, if anything, philosophy is good for." The difference between philosophers who think they know the answer to this question and the ones who do not is that the for the latter intellectual and moral progress is not a matter of getting closer to an antecedent reality but of overcoming the past. As Rorty explained, the past can only be surpassed if we acknowledge that "human beings do not have a nature to be understood, but rather a history to be reinterpreted."[36]

This is why the aim of his most important book, *Philosophy and the Mirror of Nature*, was to undermine the reader's confidence "in 'the mind' as something about which one should have a 'philosophical' view, in 'knowledge' as something about which there ought be a 'theory' and which has 'foundations,' and in 'philosophy' as it has been conceived since Kant." Instead, for Rorty, the only moral concern of Western philosophers should be to continue the conversation of the West rather than insisting upon the priority of and solutions for the traditional problems of modern philosophy. Against epistemology's ongoing search for a common ground in notions as diverse as Being, forms, and language, hermeneutics instead "sees the relation between various discourses as those of strands in a possible conversation, a conversation which presupposes no disciplinary matrix which unites the speakers, but where the hope of agreement is never lost so long as the conversation lasts."[37] But how can hermeneutics provide a philosophy without disciplinary matrices, common grounds, and methods? In the Synergos Seminars at George Mason University in 1982 Rorty declared that hermeneutics is not only linguistic but also essentially anti-Platonic and therefore capable of overcoming our epistemological tradition:

> What Nietzsche – and, more generally, "hermeneutics" – has to tell us is not that we need a new method, but rather that we should look askance at the idea of method. He and his followers should not be viewed as offering us a new set of concepts, but rather as offering a certain skepticism about all possible concepts, including the ones they themselves use ... they should be seen as urging us to think of concepts as tools rather than pictures – problem-solving instruments rather than firm foundations from which to criticize those who use different concepts.[38]

So hermeneutics for Rorty is not a method or discipline to deploy in order to achieve the results that epistemology and metaphysics always failed to reach but rather a demonstration of why we should no longer attempt to achieve them in the first place. "Hermeneutics is his name for the discipline which he commends to us as the successor, what philosophers will concern themselves with once the mirroring notion has lost its grip."[39] Thus, from "the educational, as opposed to the epistemological or the technological, point of view, the way things are said is more important than the possession of truths."[40] It should not come as a surprise that Rorty often defined hermeneutics as the "struggle against" truth, which is always contingent and historical. It is precisely in this struggle that the anarchic vein of the Rorty's hermeneutics emerges as a resistance to analytic philosophy. In order to understand this vein it is necessary to outline how Kuhn and Gadamer influenced his position: Kuhn's theory of scientific revolutions allowed Rorty to understand analytic philosophy as just another dominant paradigm waiting to be replaced, and Gadamer's notion of *Bildung* represented the appropriate alternative to "knowledge" as the goal of thinking.

Kuhn, who acknowledged the hermeneutic nature of his own theory, provided Rorty with the arguments and justifications he would use to resist analytic philosophy. Kuhn showed not only how dominant paradigms always seem to their practitioners as the final framework, when in fact they are contingent, but also how they are replaced. This replacement takes place when universally recognized scientific achievements, which had provided the model of problems, methods, and solutions for a community of scientists, reach a crisis. Such crises, which Rorty also diagnosed within analytic philosophy, become evident in those anomalies and discrepancies that resist the expected solutions of normal scientific experiments and make progress impossible. Kuhn "questioned whether philosophy of science could construct an algorithm for choice among scientific theories," and Rorty also doubted "whether epistemology could, starting from science, work its way outward to the rest of culture by discovering the common ground of as much of human discourse as could be thought of as 'cognitive' or 'rational.'"[41] It is also important to stress that Kuhn led Rorty to think about the ways in which analytic dominance of the field might reflect contingent social and historical circumstances.

The Gadamerian notion of *Bildung* is particularly important for Rorty because it provided the possibility of philosophizing without being tied to the epistemological dream of analytic philosophy. Translated as "edification," *Bildung* is not meant only to substitute for our notion of knowledge but also to take up the "hermeneutic activity of making connections between our own culture and some exotic culture or historical period, or between our own discipline and another discipline which seems to pursue incommensurable aims in an incommensurable vocabulary." In this way edifying discourses for Rorty become "abnormal" in Kuhn's meaning of the term because they "take us out of our old selves by the power of strangeness, to aid us in becoming new beings." The epistemological dream of achieving indubitable knowledge becomes secondary to finding new ways of becoming different, expressing ourselves, and interpreting the world. In sum, through *Bildung* we finally become aware that the quest for truth is only one among many ways in which we might be edified and that "there is no normal philosophical discourse which provides common commensurating ground" to evaluate other philosophies or

> for those who see science and edification as, respectively, "rational" and "irrational," and those who see the quest for objectivity as one possibility among others to be taken account of in *wirkungsgeschichtliche Bewusstsein*. If there is no such common ground, all we can do is to show how the other side looks from our own point of view. That is, all we can do is be hermeneutic about the opposition – trying to show how the odd or paradoxical or offensive things they say hang together with the rest of what they want to say, and how what they say looks when put in our own alternative idiom. This sort of hermeneutics with polemical intent is common to Heidegger's and Derrida's attempts to deconstruct the tradition.⁴²

It is important to point out that Rorty does not hide the "polemical intent" of his hermeneutics, that is, the "struggle" against normal discourses and common grounds in science and philosophy. This polemical intent, which was also present in some analytical philosophers in the sixties and seventies, is a common feature in many European thinkers whom he admired and probably also wanted to imitate. Although Rorty always presented himself as a proud American philosopher, this did not stop his US colleagues from seeing in him as the personification of the European intellectual. This arose from Rorty's call for the abandonment of analytic philosophy for a more pluralistic, historical, and hermeneutic approach. This suggestion was not only philosophically polemical but also antiscientific because Rorty, like Vattimo, was worried by analytic philosophy's scientific bent: "The history of philosophy is punctuated by revolts against the practices of previous philosophers and by attempts to transform philosophy into science – a discipline in which universally recognized decision-procedures are available for testing philosophical thesis."⁴³

Rorty decided to participate in one of these revolts not simply for theoretical reasons – his belief that metaphysical philosophy had run its course – but also because of cultural and educational concerns that arose from analytical philosophy's inability to recognize a plurality of positions. Even though a Anglo-American analytic philosophy had digested the linguistic turn, it failed to understand what it meant for those problems (realism, representationalism, subjectivism) that characterized the discipline. This failure is evident in the difference between analytical philosophers who use the linguistic turn to dismiss traditional philosophical problems and continental thinkers who refuse to accept that its benefits were so straightforward. While both agree on the philosophical significance of language, they disagree over its capacity to solve problems. Rorty distinguish these groups as "argumentative/systematic" and "emblematic/edifying" philosophers.

> Some philosophers, like Quine or Sellars or Gödel or Gettier, show something which one can repeat. They attain an objective result ... Other philosophers are emblematic, and are known for a vocabulary, for having invented a new language-game, rather than having made a famous move in an old one ... The one sort of philosopher is associated with the notion of "objectivity" and science-as-a-model-for-philosophy. The other is associated with the man of letters.[44]

Analytic philosophers, who for the most part rely on formal logic in measuring and solving problems, conquered the American academy in the 1960s and 1970s because of two factors: the discipline's epistemological obsession and the political circumstances of the epoch. The reduction of philosophy to mere linguistic and logical analysis proved to be a valuable political cover, a way of denying any dangerous political opinions when any suggestion of such could be enough to keep an intellectual from the economic and career security of a tenured appointment. In order to protect themselves from the taint of controversy, American philosophers turned away from the world of political and cultural debate and focused on the pursuit of objective truths by employing methods of physicists, biologists, and mathematicians. Although positivism had established itself as an important movement on the American philosophical scene well before 1960s, its emphasis on rigour and problem solving fit with the culture of the American university at the time.[45]

This situation led to analytical philosophers controlling the American Philosophical Association's policies, rankings, and other significant resources. Philosophy departments where analytical philosophers predominated ranked higher in reputational surveys, and journals devoted to analytic work were better regarded. Nonanalysts were looked down upon by their analytic colleagues. In a report drafted in 1979, Rorty pointed out that analytic philosophers, "who make up most of the membership of the Program Committees, tend to have ... suspicions about Whiteheadians, Deweyans, or phenomenologists, not to mention bright young admirers of Deleuze or Gadamer ... [and these] feel that the chances of their papers getting on the program are so small that they don't bother to submit them."[46] The suspicions of analytical philosophers were no longer philosophical but political; students, researchers, and professors were dismissed for working on nonanalytical authors.

This problem was at the centre of the "pluralistic revolt" when Rorty was president of the Eastern Division of the APA in 1979. The revolt, as Neil Gross recalls, centred around the demand of continental philosophers not only to move the association in a more pluralistic direction but also to allow them to serve in leadership capacities.[47] Although Rorty was already an object of suspicion to analytical philosophers – *Philosophy and the Mirror of Nature*, his most influential book, appeared the same year – once he decided to raise this issue at meetings, they became furious. In order to move the association in a more pluralistic direction Rorty attempted to call into question many of its dogmas, such as the standard interpretation of the linguistic turn. Analytic philosophers rejected not only the possibility of paradigm change but also different philosophical voices, problems, and traditions in order to cling to positivist hopes for a scientific philosophy that could solve all problems once for all. It should not come as a surprise that Rorty invited his fellow analytical philosophers to take a "relaxed attitude" toward the question of logical rigour and to "let a hundred flowers bloom" as hermeneutic philosophers do.[48]

Vattimo and Rorty demonstrate the practical and polemical tone that interpretation can acquire once we resist political or philosophical impositions. Both reject truth in favour of democracy and freedom. For Vattimo the "farewell to truth is the commencement, and the very basis, of democracy," and for Rorty, when you "take care of freedom, truth will take care of itself." It is important to remember that Vattimo and Rorty do not believe their hermeneutic resistances to truth will solve our problems, but they might allow us to get a sense of everyone's existential right to interpret differently. The anarchic vein that runs through their hermeneutics stances – as a vital "practice" and "struggle" – not only resists technological globalization and analytic philosophy but also shows the existential effort that interpretation always requires. This effort, as we will see, was also necessary for those who had deploy interpretation in order to transgress objective views of the psyche.

INTERPRETATION AND TRANSGRESSION

Although interpretation is a central concept in the thought of Freud and Nietzsche, they are not ordinarily considered hermeneutic thinkers. Heidegger regarded Nietzsche as the "last metaphysician" and did not have a high opinion of Freud. Gadamer briefly mentions Freud and Nietzsche in his writings but always resisted including them within the history of philosophical hermeneutics. Surprisingly, it is Ricoeur, also known for his conservative positions, who made the effort to incorporate them. In order to present their theory of interpretation, the French philosopher refers to Freud and Nietzsche as two (along with Marx) of the great "masters of suspicion." He coined this expression to identify a negative moment in the process of interpretation where meaning was reduced to the manifestation of the subterranean will to power (Nietzsche), unconscious (Freud), and class interests (Marx). Although these thinkers practised a hermeneutics of "suspicion" or "depth," where claims to truth and unmediated contact with reality are debunked in order to assert the need for interpretation, some critics wonder whether Ricoeur's operation was conditioned by the new current of structuralism in France in the early 1960s.[49] Whatever Ricoeur's intentions, his effort to stress these different thinkers' theories of interpretation helped broaden hermeneutics beyond Gadamer's canon.

The goal of this section is not to justify Freud's and Nietzsche's place in the history of hermeneutics, which is now largely acknowledged, but rather to outline the anarchic vein that runs through their theories of interpretation. This vein is evident in the transgressions they committed against in their respective fields, psychology and philology. Freud created psychoanalysis, where the "interpretation of dreams is the royal road to a knowledge of the unconscious activities of the mind." And Nietzsche developed an existential project for which "there are no facts, but only interpretations" at the service of the will to power. As Élisabeth Roudinesco points out, psychoanalysis was "an act of transgression, a way of surreptitiously listening to words, taking them in without seeming to hear them or define them. A bizarre discipline, a fragile combination uniting soul and body, affect and reason, politics and animality."[50] Although the same cannot be said of Nietzsche, as he did not create a new discipline, his was also an act of transgression as he called upon the revaluation of values and the abandonment of the God hypothesis and all its metaphysical substitutes. The anarchic vein of their hermeneutics, once again appealing to Schürmann's and Critchley's definitions of anarchy, is apparent in their transgressions against the received wisdoms of their disciplines but also in the "different way of conceiving and enacting social relations between people" that they put in practice. What defines these new relations, as we will see, is the "free agreement" among people instead of a system or rule.

According to Dilthey's famous distinction between natural sciences (*Naturwissenschaften*) and spiritual sciences (*Geisteswissenschaften*), psychoanalysis (also called "depth psychology" and "psychology of the deeper layers") should be placed among the former where a system or rule explains natural processes in terms of cause and effect. While Freud would agree with this characterization – he always presented himself as a scientist and psychoanalysis as a natural science – its hypotheses are retrospective and cannot be used for predictions as in the laboratory practices of chemistry and physics. Freud's insistence on presenting psychoanalysis as a natural science has both biographical and sociological roots that will also elucidate the role of interpretation in his thought.

Freud was a scientist and a physician, animated by a scientific and therapeutic ambition, who carried out research into cerebral paralysis and neuroanatomy before turning toward the practice of medical psychopathology. After attempting to relieve symptoms of hysteria through hypnosis and the cathartic method – suggested by the neurologist Jean-Martin Charcot and in collaboration with the physician Josep Breuer – he began to apply the technical method of "free associations," where patients are encouraged to talk freely about their memories, fantasies, and problems. As a medical man, Freud's original hope was to discover not only the cause of neurotic symptoms but also their treatment by facilitating the patient's recollection of the deviations of her infantile development. This treatment was meant to be comparable with the treatment of any other physical illness: just as tubercle bacilli could be regarded as the cause of pulmonary tuberculosis and abolished by a strict treatment regimen, so neuroses were caused by repressed infantile impulses and abolished by recalling those impulses. Thus, Freud defined psychoanalysis as

> the name (1) of a procedure for the investigation of mental processes which are almost inaccessible in any other way, (2) of a method (based upon that investigation) for the treatment of neurotic disorders and (3) of a collection of psychological information obtained along those lines, which is gradually being accumulated into a new scientific discipline.[51]

In order to understand why Freud presented psychoanalysis as "a new scientific discipline" it is important to recall that Darwin's ideas on evolution and the descent of man were being newly accepted throughout the scientific communities in the West at the time. Humanity was no longer viewed as a special creation but simply as the most highly evolved primate. Psychology could not base itself anymore upon man's spiritual qualities or conditioned reflexes but only upon those biological and sexual drives that motivate the behaviour of both humans and animals. In order to work as a successful treatment, psychoanalysis could not depart from the criteria of science and had to participate in the positivist scientific culture of the early twentieth century. This implied that its foundations were in biology, chemistry, and other natural sciences and that it could be regarded as a technique that could be learned like any other medical treatment, which placed the psychoanalyst in the traditional role of a skilled physician.

Freud intended his work to "furnish a psychology that shall be a natural science: that is, to represent psychical processes as qualitatively determinate states of specifiable material particles."[52] It should not come as a surprise that Freud sometimes compares the work of the chemist with that of the analyst: while the former "isolates the fundamental substance, the chemical 'element,' out of the salt in which it had been combined with other elements and in which it was unrecognizable," the latter informs the patient how and why his pathological manifestations emerge.[53]

The problem of linking this practice to the natural sciences, as Anthony Storr points out, is that many "have failed to appreciate the importance of psychoanalysis as a hermeneutic system and as a way of looking at human nature."[54] Although his therapeutic project was meant to be a science of the psyche, transgressing the field of psychology through a Darwinian lens, it also embraced a number of features from humanities, religion, and the arts. The riddle of neurosis, for example, was also solved by relying on "the Hebrew Bible and the Greek tragedies, archaeology and sculpture, and everyday or 'folk' understandings of psychology. Ultimately, Freud fused all these currents into a powerful synthesis, neither wholly scientific nor wholly humanistic."[55] This explains the contrasting views of psychologists (who saw psychoanalysis as putting the very principle of psychology in danger), scientists (who thought it belonged to literature), and philosophers (as it resembled a strange psychology). Psychoanalysis became a movement rather than a simple medical treatment for neurosis both because it was rejected by many academic disciplines and because of it claims to explain too many matters of the human psyche. But why and how has hermeneutics contributed in this enterprise?

Although Freud does not refer to the term "hermeneutics" in his writings, there is little doubt he knew about its methods through the exegesis of the Torah that was part of his religious education.[56] This is evident in his use of the term *Deutung*, "interpretation," which was particularly provocative for a medical physician to employ considering that in German it was also used in the context of divination and astrology in addition to the explication of concealed meanings in biblical and juridical texts. But as a theory of textual interpretation, in particular biblical texts, hermeneutics was also conceived as a theory of knowledge whose insights exceed those of the simple elucidation of texts. This is probably why Freud felt authorized to coin the term "interpretative art" to refer to psychoanalysis. But as an "interpretative art," psychoanalysis surpasses the boundaries of hermeneutics not only as a theory of textual interpretation but also as a theory of knowledge, considering the radically different nature of its objects of investigation: neuroses, dreams, and unconscious conflicts that dominate our mental lives.

The different nature of these objects of investigation, as Philippe Cabestan points out, indicates that for Freud "understanding or comprehension is not based on empathy, which would suppose a direct identification with the other, but can only be attained by interpretation."[57] If interpretation is the only way to understand the gap between what is conscious and unconscious, that is, to overcome the repression that prevents the awareness of deeply rooted neuroses, it's because they can be neither biologically explained nor immediately observed and analyzed. This explains why Freud gives so much attention to features that are not usually noticed, such as random movements, slips of the tongue, and lapses. While there are a number of examples in his writings of these features – such as the important chapter "Forgetting of Proper Names" in *Psychopathology of Everyday Life* (1901) – its fullest expression is in *The Interpretation of Dreams* (*Die Traumdeutung*, 1900), where dreams are presented as "the royal road to a knowledge of the unconscious activities of the mind." But what differentiates psychoanalytic interpretations from other interpretation methodologies of the dream?

> Every attempt that has hitherto been made to solve the problem of dreams has dealt directly with their *manifest* content as it is presented in our memory. All such attempts have endeavored to arrive at an interpretation of dreams from their manifest content or (if no interpretation was attempted) to form a judgement as to their nature on the basis of that manifest content. We are alone in taking something else into account. We have introduced a new class of physical material between the manifest content of dreams and the conclusion of our enquiry: namely, their *latent* content, or (as we say) the "dream-thoughts," arrived at by means of our procedure. It is from these dream-thoughts and not from a dream's manifest content that we disentangle its meaning. We are thus presented with a new task which had no previous existence: the task, that is, of investigating the relations between the manifest content of dreams and the latent dream-thoughts, and of tracing out the processes by which the latter have been changed into the former.[58]

The distinction between the manifest (the dream itself as it is remembered) and the latent content of a dream (its hidden meaning) is only the starting point of Freud's process as what these dreams repress is also an important part of the analysis. While Freud described manifest dreams "as a disguised fulfillment of repressed wishes," that is, of all the wishes that are linked with our sexual life, such as masochism, exhibitionism, or the Oedipus complex, their meanings can only be attained through interpretation given the different symbolism at stake. This is why against the traditional "dream book" mode of interpretation in terms of fixed symbols he applied "free association," which obliged the patient (not the interpreter) to report hidden or forgotten thoughts. As Freud explains, the "patient's symptoms and pathological manifestations, like all his mental activities, are of a highly composite kind; the elements of this compound are at bottom motives, instinctual impulses. But the patient knows nothing of these elementary motives or not nearly enough. We teach him to understand the way in which these highly complicated mental formations are compounded."[59]

Independent of Freud's insistence on presenting psychoanalysis as "a new scientific discipline," there is no doubt that his psychological revolution was (indirectly) set in motion in order to overcome the imposed facts of the positivist scientific culture of the early twentieth century. Like other hermeneutical projects, one of his chief targets was the empiricist theory of modern science, which conceived the human mind as a tabula rasa, a blank surface inscribed by experience and subject to description. This scientific understanding of the mind, common also to Descartes, presupposed certain moral values that were supposed to find a correlative in the social world the mind inhabited; in other words, objectivity prevailed over the subject, which was considered merely a mirror of nature.

Against these common beliefs of modern science, Freud suggested that our actions are motivated not by pure, rational, and logical mechanisms but rather by many different unknown forces, motives, and impulses constantly clashing within and between our conscious and unconscious minds. For these reasons, familiar forms of irrational behaviour such as self-deception, depression, or even childhood masturbation, all of which were problematic in the Cartesian model of invisible unitary consciousness and as well as nineteenth-century medical practices, became in Freud part of the normal life of human beings. Freud anarchically transgressed the accepted demarcation between the "rational/normal" and the "irrational/abnormal" human being.

However, Freud did not limit his discoveries to explaining the normality of the "abnormal," which by itself produced great progress for civilization. He also emphasized how the dynamically interchangeable relation between the conscious and the subconscious is the same as that between the human being and his society. In this structure, problems might emerge from the oppression of instincts (imposed from without by society), from unconscious determinations (death or sexual drives upwelling from within), or from their objective interpretations, in other words, from the positivist psychologies of the time. These psychologies held that a patient's suffering came only from objective ignorance, in other words, from a lack of information about his own life. If this were actually true, then a better description of the patient's dreams would be enough to cure him. But, as we've seen, the mind implies unconscious features that not only determine conscious ones but also reject the expression of certain mental states. In this condition, interpretation is required to inform the patient of those memories he has repressed.

The transgression that Freud brought about by outlining unconscious mental processes and the analysis of the human psyche through the vital exercise of interpretation spread irreversible doubts about the objective formation of human rationality. Although his "art of interpretation" invalidated positivist psychology, which often categorized psychic illnesses without ever listening to the patient, he failed to see that his doctrine carried with it "a politics, a philosophy, an ideology, an anthropology, and a movement toward emancipation. Nothing was more contrary to the spirit of psychoanalysis than to disguise it as a so-called positive science and to keep it apart from all political commitment."[60] If freedom is an essential condition for social relations to prosper without personal and social restraints Freud should have disclosed his doctrine progressive nature. This is probably why until Ricoeur he was not considered a hermeneutic thinker and his project was interpreted as a development and radicalization of the previous psychological hermeneutics of Schleiermacher and Dilthey. These thinkers also doubted that the author of a work would be able to reconstruct its meaning if informed of all the techniques used to produce it. Just as a complete reconstruction of a patient's life would not necessarily solve his problems, the history of the production of a work of art could not explain the meaning of the work to the author.

The anarchic vein of Freud's "art of interpretation" is evident not only when he overcomes the boundaries of hermeneutics as a theory of textual interpretation and as a theory of knowledge but also through the presence of Nietzsche in his work. When Thomas Mann portrayed Freud as an heir of Nietzsche he felt uncomfortable in being related to such a radical thinker, even though there is plenty of evidence that Nietzsche anticipated many of psychoanalytic intuitions and was a strong presence in Freud's life.[61] For example, in a meeting of the Vienna Psychoanalytic Society on 28 October 1908, devoted to the analysis of *Ecce Homo*, Ernest Jones reported that Freud several times referred to Nietzsche as the man who "had a more penetrating knowledge of himself than any other man who ever lived or was likely to live."[62] And in 1925 Freud referred to him as "another philosopher whose guesses and intuitions often agree in the most astonishing way with the laborious findings of psycho-analysis, was for a long time avoided by me on that very account: I was less concerned with the question of priority than with keeping my mind unembarrassed."[63]

A number of scholars believe Nietzsche's presence in Freud's work is attributable to the broad intellectual forces of the period that influenced both men (Darwin, contemporary theories of energy, and earlier psychological studies such as those of Hippolyte Taine) and to their common interests (Greek tragedy, Goethe, and pathological states), but the truth lies in Nietzsche's psychological intuitions beyond the boundaries of natural sciences. While Freud was reluctant to admit that psychoanalysis was based more in fantasy than in facts, Nietzsche had no doubts that the will to knowledge (independent of the object of inquiry) was always linked to imagination. This is why, instead of psychoanalysis's simplistic theories of instincts (ultimately reduced to sexuality and death), Nietzsche provided a vocabulary for highly nuanced instinctive drives at the margins of the unconscious.

Nietzsche referred to himself in many places as the "new psychologist" of the West and complained in 1888 that no one had yet characterized him "als Psychologe." This complaint is based on his belief and discovery that humans are creatures whose real natures are unknown to themselves, in other words, we "are unknown to ourselves, we men of knowledge – and with good reason. We have never sought ourselves – how could it happen that we should ever *find* ourselves?"⁶⁴ Psychology, according to the German thinker, can disclose our true nature and lead us to the genuine roots of our creative powers. But the problem of these powers is that they are not only hidden behind ideologies, metaphysics, and dogmas but also dependent on external and internal deceptions. Why do we constantly believe in transcendental agencies instead of freely relying on and creating ourselves?

Although Nietzsche is aware that his psychological method alone is unable to successfully freeze the need for metaphysical consolation and support, it can address the "psychic needs of humans, easing the burden of our life, giving us peace of mind and 'cooling' us."⁶⁵ This is an important insight considering every metaphysics is always subsequently shattered by the collapse of the system that it provided, resulting in a state of discontent, repression, and scepticism. Against these states Nietzsche prescribes to "cool down" our devotion to metaphysical drives, that is, those intellectual beliefs that indirectly serve to satisfy certain powerful psychic needs. As we can see, psychology serves to freeze those metaphysical needs that are never satisfied by metaphysics itself; that is, it offers a sort of "existential salvation precisely by redeeming us from our need for salvation. The salvation from salvation was to become a central motif of Nietzsche's mature philosophy."⁶⁶

According to Walter Kaufmann and Robert B. Pippin the psychological aspects of Nietzsche's thought are no less significant than the philosophical ones.⁶⁷ Although eminent interpreters of the German thinker – such as Gilles Deleuze, Sarah Kofman, and Arthur C. Danto – would not agree, there is significant evidence in his writings to support this position. For example, in paragraph 23 of *Beyond Good and Evil*, Nietzsche demands that "psychology again be recognized as the queen of the sciences, and that the rest of the sciences exist to serve and prepare for it. Because, from now on, psychology is again the path to the most fundamental problems." Even though there are many other statements we could refer to justify Kaufman's and Pippin's positions, and therefore Freud interest in Nietzsche, Eric Blondel is right when he states that

> Nietzsche can nonetheless be considered as a psychologist ... insofar as he tries to treat his reader not only as a reader, as an intellect, but as a living person, as a psychological human being, whose feelings, violence, affects, values, will to power can be aroused, stimulated, transformed by the act of reading – which is also an expression of the will to power, not a simple act of the mind, but a movement of the muscles, of the drives and of the affects, of the will, that is to say: an interpretation.[68]

The reason Nietzsche does not treat his readers with the therapist's benevolent neutrality is because writing and interpretation are not speculative activities but rather expressions of the will to power. Author and interpreter are always involved in a psychological situation where power and affects emerge; that is, their existential condition is at stake. As we can see, psychology assisted Nietzsche in carrying out an existential project to evoke a mood of suspicion and distrust toward dogmatic views founded on metaphysics. But what role does interpretation play in this existential project?

In order to outline the anarchic vein of Nietzsche's hermeneutics it is necessary to understand his departure from philology, both as a discipline and academic position, and also his opposition to positivism, which Freud confronted as well.

In 1869, even before concluding his doctoral dissertation, Nietzsche won the chair in classical philology at the University of Basel through the support of the great philologist Friedrich Ritschl. Two years later, at the age of twenty-seven, he published *The Birth of Tragedy from the Spirit of Music* which is at once a reinterpretation of ancient Greece, a critique of contemporary culture, and a program to revitalize it. This text, together with his lectures, were, among other things, an expression of his doubts about the value of his discipline. According to Nietzsche, the academy was responsible for rendering the study of antiquity a purely antiquarian activity, which created a gulf between the philologist and the beauty of the Greek world. How could philologists remind us of this world if their discipline was no longer capable of regarding antiquity as a model worth imitating, in other words, as much more than an accumulation of artifacts for academic investigation?

In order to transgress the accepted academic parameters of philology Nietzsche emphasizes not only the primacy of philosophy over philology – "What was philology has now been made into philosophy" – but also its hermeneutic nature as he invokes it's artistic components. "Philology is part natural science, part history, part art, in the end, method. Art inasmuch as it aspires to a clarified comprehension of antiquity."[69] Art becomes necessary to grasp the irrationality that lies at the bottom of classical culture and civilization. The goal is to "bring to light the irrationality of human things, without any embarrassment – that is the goal of our brothers and companions." In order to bring to light this irrationality, as well as to reconstitute its broad meanings, the philologist must first overcome his discipline's analytical character, which causes it to lose all the interconnectedness of his investigation. This is why Nietzsche regarded his colleagues as a mere "factory hand[s] in the service of science" who have lost their taste for "embracing any larger totality, or bringing different points of view into existence."[70] If interpretation can bring these different views into existence, then Nietzsche, as Babette Babich points out, went on "to offer a hermeneutic reading of classical philology beyond what he calls the mechanical or 'automatic' notion of history."[71]

Before venturing into Nietzsche's opposition to positivism it's important to point out how his departure from philology did not in fact unfold only on a methodological territory but also in its relation to history. While academic philology relied on a "mechanical or automatic history," aimed at an objective reconstruction of history, Nietzsche calls for history in the service of life, that is, associated with freedom and emancipation. This is why in the second Untimely Meditation, "On the Uses and Disadvantages of

History for Life" (1874), he refers to a "historical disease" that had overrun late-nineteenth-century Europe. A person afflicted with this disease wanders like a tourist among the different ages, embodies any character, and disguises himself in the style he pleases so that history acquires a paralyzing power. The problem in objectifying the past in this manner is that one ends up by forgetting oneself in the attempt to give an eyewitness account of history. While this is what occurs in "monumental history" (viewing the past as providing examples of human glory) and "antiquarian history" (retrieving the past for the its own sake), there is a third mode that Nietzsche approves of:

> It becomes clear how necessary it is to mankind to have, beside the monumental and antiquarian modes of regarding the past, a *third* mode, the *critical*: and this, too, in the service of life. If he is to live, man must possess and from time to time employ the strength to break up and dissolve a part of the past: he does this by bringing it before the tribunal, scrupulously examining it and finally condemning it; every past, however, is worthy to be condemned ... It is not justice which here sits in judgement; it is even less mercy which pronounces the verdict; it is life alone, that dark, driving power that insatiably thirsts for itself.[72]

The fact that the past is judged in terms of life in "critical history" puts an end to the heritage of universal history and to mirroring the past. Against the excess of historical knowledge without an adequate capacity for original creation, Nietzsche calls for a historical act that creates historical innovation and avoids cultural decadence.

The problem for Nietzsche now (who retired from teaching in 1876 not only for health reasons but also because of his intellectual break with academic philology) is that nineteenth-century modernity has come to play a destructive role in the European historical-cultural continuity. The fact that at the peak of the tradition of universal history that very history comes to an end and discloses its own unacknowledged driving engine – the will to power – is extremely important for Nietzsche. In the modern world, as he wrote in a famous aphorism, "the real world" becomes "fable," and truth is abolished, "The true world – we have abolished. What world has remained? The apparent one perhaps? But no! *With the true world we have also abolished the apparent one.*" Contrary to what one might expect, it is not the real world of traditional metaphysics that has become fable but rather, as Vattimo has explained, "the world as such, in which a distinction between true and false is no longer operable, that is fable in its deepest structure."[73] If the world as such has become fable and history reduced to a progressive disclosure of an energy as will to power instead of an universal history, what is the role of interpretation now?

For Nietzsche, to interpret does not mean to search and analyze a historical object and its meaning but rather to carry on an energetic activity, in other words, to advance the energies that increase the power of life. This power will increase or decrease depending on an intensity that also functions as a criterion for interpretation. But if a change in power is necessarily followed by a change in interpretation, what is the ultimate point of reference? In order to respond to this question Nietzsche claims that everything is interpretation and that the subjectivity of the interpreter is not an ultimate point of reference. In this manner both the historicist and positivist approach are overcome because it is up to the interpreter to confer meaning on the past. But interpretation must not be thought of as an action of a subject since this is already the result of an interpretation determined by a contest of energies and interests. This is why "against positivism, which stops at phenomena, 'we have only facts,'" Nietzsche says:

> No, facts is precisely what there is not, only interpretations. We cannot establish any fact "in itself": perhaps it is folly to want to do such a thing. "Everything is subjective," you say; but even this is interpretation. The "subject" is not something given, it is something added and invented and projected

behind what there is. – Finally, is it necessary to posit an interpreter behind the interpretation? Even this is invention, hypothesis.[74]

Several interpreters believe Nietzsche's opposition to positivism derives from his knowledge of the psychology of sensation, a cognitive discipline that invokes illusory experiences, while others think it's part of his perspectivism, where there are no uninterpreted facts or truths. The former base their views on his proximity to psychology; the latter on the way he characterized the thought of his final creative period. The problem of describing Nietzsche's opposition to positivism in these forms is that interpretation ceases to be a vital part of his existential project. In order to understand the anarchic role interpretation plays for Nietzsche, it is necessary to recall the specific difference between "perspective" (*Perspektive*) and "interpretation" (*Auslegung, Ausdeutung*).

Human beings are situated at a particular point in space and time that inevitably limits their capacity for knowledge, making it impossible to have objective and disinterested observation of reality. Evaluations for Nietzsche are possible only from three basic types of perspective ("physiological," "instinctual," and "sociohistorical") that place certain limits on what human beings can know. As Alan Schrift points out, "Whereas our perspectives are ... 'determined' and outside our control, the form which we give to these perspectives, the interpretation which we as will to power construct with them, is not."[75] Interpretation clarifies and completes perspective, but it also imparts a new orientation to the problem of knowledge and existence. While perspectivism is framed within images that are tied to the perceptual sphere, interpretation is connected to categories of images that require a creative initiative lacking in the former. But how does this creative initiative take place?

> Generally, however, correct perception – that is to say, the adequate expression of an object in a subject – strikes me as something contradictory and impossible; for between two such absolutely different spheres as subject and object there

is no causality, no correctness, no expression, but at most an aesthetic comportment, by which I mean a suggestive rendering, a stammering translation into an altogether foreign language. Though even that would require a freely poetic and freely inventive intermediate sphere and mediating force.⁷⁶

The freedom Nietzsche refers to in this passage is particularly evident in translators and historians, who, even when their task demands a personal effort to discover adequate equivalences between two languages or reconstruct the past, are called interpreters. If no one assumes a translation or reconstruction to be absolutely faithful to an original text, it's because interpretation introduces a coefficient of subjectivity, that is, of energy, invention, and originality. "Now, far from constituting some simple addition to reality, this coefficient makes reality appear even more true than when directly perceived."⁷⁷

These examples demonstrate not only how interpretation supposes some creative initiative on the part of the interpreter, which is required by the very nature of the object of investigation, but also the impracticality of gathering together different viewpoints into a superior synthesis. This is why "to grasp everything," for Nietzsche means to grasp nothing, to misapprehend the nature of knowledge. In the absence of any organ for "knowledge" about the world, the anarchic vein of interpretation (energy, originality, and creation) becomes vital to increase the power of life.

Freud's and Nietzsche's transgressions of psychology and philology through interpretation involved risk for their careers but also for their theories. Freud was forced to create a movement to ensure psychoanalysis's legacy, and Nietzsche's departure from the academy required greater efforts to publish and promote his ideas. Although neither used the term "hermeneutics" to refer to their intuitions, interpretation played a central role in their transgressions as their opposition to positivism demonstrates. This opposition required an anarchic gesture both to break free from positivism's authority within the scientific culture of their epoch and to ignore those irrational or abnormal features vital to a freer existence. These – Freud's "free associations" and Nietzsche's "free inventions" – can only be managed in the absence of systems, rules, and methods given their unconscious roots. But what role does interpretation play when the goal of hermeneutics is to create change?

INTERPRETATION AND ALTERATION

Although Martin Luther and St Augustine occupy important places in the history of hermeneutics for their contributions to biblical interpretation, the former had the greatest influence because of the revolutionary role interpretation played in his principle of the "sola scriptura" and his translation of the Bible. With Luther's impact in Germany comparable to if not greater than that of Dante in Italy or Rousseau in France, Hegel could affirm that if Luther had done nothing besides this translation, he would still be one of the greatest benefactors of the German-speaking people. But Augustine, who is considered one of the most important theologians in the history of Christianity for his adaptation of classical thought to Christian teaching, deeply influenced both Heidegger and Gadamer. Heidegger found in Augustine the most important "source for his conception of the enacted meaning [*Vollzugsinn*] of statements, a conception he deployed against the tradition of metaphysical idealism," and Gadamer ascribed the universal claim of hermeneutics to his idea of "inner conversation."[78]

Luther and Augustine, unlike the transgressive author pairs I have already explored, lived in different centuries. But they share similar concerns about the role interpretation can play in the translation and the sacralization of the Bible which always include strong semantic and conceptual alterations of the original meaning. It must be pointed out that Luther was part the Order of Saint Augustine and cited his writings more than any other nonscriptural source. The goal of this section is to venture into the anarchic vein of these two thinkers' biblical hermeneutics and practice of interpretation. This vein, independent of the significant differences between them, consists in alterations their interpretations created or disclosed through practice. Alterations, like resistances and transgressions, are not "driven by a grand

and unified rule" but rather are a result of "practice" in line with Schürmann's and Critchley's definition of anarchy. This element of practice was central for Luther's challenge to ecclesiastical authorities and Augustine's *spiritualizing* of sacred and pagan texts not only for the alterations they produced but also for the freedom they strived for.

Luther's challenge of the ecclesiastical authorities was an act of freedom because it demonstrated, as Gadamer points out, that neither "the doctrinal authority of the Pope nor the appeal to tradition can obviate the work of hermeneutics, which can safeguard the reasonable meaning of a text against all imposition."[79] This imposition, which forced every believer to turn to officials for readings, interpretations, and elucidations of the Bible, was contested by Luther in his *Ninety-Five Theses* (1517) and his translation of the Bible into German (1534). Against spiritual, cultural, and political dominion, Luther believed that the literal meaning of the Bible contained its own proper spiritual significance, which should be interpreted by each believer. In asserting this, the Bible Professor of Wittenberg was valorizing both the linguistic text and personal linguistic practice, the interpreter's capacity to judge for herself. In order to understand Luther's hermeneutic revolution – which eventually split the thousand-year-old Roman Catholic Church in two – it's necessary to clarify how he altered the sacred text and what drove him to challenge the ecclesiastical authorities in the first place.

With the 500th anniversary in 2017 a number of biographies and articles have appeared to recall, among other things, what drove Luther to send his *Ninety-Five Theses* to the local archbishop and (allegedly) nail them to the door of the Wittenberg Castle church. The problem for the thirty-three-year-old Augustinian friar was the church practice of selling indulgences, which supposedly reduced the amount of time sinners had to spend in purgatory before being admitted to heaven. Although Luther was not the first or the only one to criticize this practice (Erasmus of Rotterdam also complained about the increasing number of ecclesial rules), he managed, as Lyndal Roper pointed out, to articulate "a long-standing position on the nature of grace that went back to St Augustine: the idea that our own good deeds can never ensure salvation, and that we must rely on God's mercy. Luther, however, alleged that the sacrament of confession was being perverted from a spiritual exercise into a monetary transaction."[80] For the young monk, the indulgence trade seems to have crystallized not only his resentment toward abuses by the church but also his own spiritual and identity crisis as he was afraid of not been judged worthy: "I did not love, yes, I hated the righteous God who punishes sinners." As we can see, Luther's theses were not simply a matter of political protest against the church but also the expression of an internal conflict he took very seriously.

The theses were not a set of nonnegotiable demands about how the church should reform itself but rather an invitation to debate publicly the unfair practice of indulgences. Although the church initially ignored the Augustinian monk, hoping the whole issue would blow over, he continued to speak forcefully against Rome's exploitation of ordinary Christians who were suffering sanctions for not paying indulgences. Against these indulgences Luther believed firmly in the principle of *sola fide for salvation* as Ephesians 2:8–9 states: "For by grace you have been saved *through faith*. And this is not your own doing; it is the gift of God, not a result of works, so that no one may boast." This, instead of the indulgences, was the only article on which the church should stand.

> It is the promises of God that make the church, and not the church that makes the promises of God. For the Word of God is incomparably superior to the church, and in this Word the church, being a creature, has nothing to decree, ordain, or make, but only to be decreed, ordained, and made. For who begets his own parent? Who first brings forth his own maker?[81]

As Christians began to rally to his cause and an opposition surged, Rome finally decided to confront the radical monk who called the church a brothel and the pope the Antichrist. The threat posed by Luther had become serious enough for Pope Leo

X to sign a bull threatening to excommunicate him if he did not appear in Rome to renounce his theses. Instead of going to Rome Luther not only burned the bull but also demanded an independent hearing, which eventually took place in April 1521. Standing before the emperor and ecclesiastical officials in Worms, Luther "refused to retract what he had written, declaring that he could not act against his conscience."[82] Although reformers had been executed for less, the ecclesiastical authorities knew they would have serious trouble if they killed him given his popularity. But how does this ecclesiastical debate relate to Luther hermeneutics?

> As the indulgence controversy escalated, however, the essentially hermeneutic character of Luther's position became increasingly apparent. Based mainly, but by no means exclusively, on his study of the Pauline writings, Luther's fundamental conviction was that changes in church practice over time had buried under multiple layers of pious works God's gracious offer to reconcile to himself all those who believed that Christ died for their redemption. The medieval church, argued Luther, had put the soteriological cart before the horse and inverted the relation of works and faith by seeking salvation in obedience to burdensome moral commands often invented by the church, rather than preaching forgiveness through Christ thus enabling works of love to flow from a person's communion with God. This perversion of the Christian faith was for Luther at bottom a problem of hermeneutics.[83]

As we can see, Luther's central role in the Reformation did not arise from his desire to reform the church as much as from his conviction that such reform depended on biblical interpretation. This is why the principle of *sola scriptura* was vital to his turn away from theology and tradition. For too long theology had ceased to be an exegetical practice based on a comprehensive understanding of the Bible and had come to rely exclusively on authoritative opinions: "interpreting the scriptures in light of Augustine rather than understanding Augustine in light of the scriptures."[84] Luther applied the same principle to tradition. It's not the Bible that needs tradition to be understood but rather the tradition that must constantly measure itself against scripture to verify its own validity. If no theology or tradition is necessary it's because "scriptura scripturae interpres," the "Scripture is its own interpreter," as well as the "source of all interpretation." Against "theologians of glory" (i.e., scholastics), who think they know God's majesty through rational evidence, Luther proposes a "theologia crucis," a theology of the cross because only "in the crucified Jesus is true theology and knowledge of God."[85]

Luther was advocating a Christological reading where Christ is the Word to which all the biblical words ultimately have reference: "Do you want to interpret well and safely, so put Christ in front of you"[86] This, Luther continues, is the true touchstone by which all books are to be judged. Although this principle was widely accepted during the Patristic period, as we will see with Augustine, Luther's repudiation of allegory and the fourfold meaning of scripture was in fact a "provocative renewal of patristic attitudes."[87]

David Jasper points out that "Luther's hermeneutic enterprise was partly made possible by an advance in technology, that is, the invention of the *printing press*."[88] Books were no longer restricted to single precious copies locked away in churches or in libraries for few to appreciate but rather were increasingly available among people of modest means and little formal learning. Together with the spread of literacy the printing press transformed the Bible into a common book for everyone to study. The fact that in medieval schools the Bible was studied as a glossed text, the *Glossa Ordinaria*, in which each verse was surrounded by commentaries handed down from the Church Fathers, always bothered Luther. Although he respected the Church Fathers insofar as they were themselves competent hermeneuts, he believed these commentaries required a *destructio*, that is, a destruction of the medieval scholastic metaphysics that covered over the original Christian message. The printing press could facilitate this enterprise.

In order to put this destruction into practice, Luther, in the winter semester of 1513–14, instructed the printer of the university to produce an edition of the Psalter for his students with wide margins and lots of white space between the lines. The goal of this edition was not simply to demand that students reproduce Luther's own commentaries and write their own but, most of all, to allow the students to experience the text without any traditional theological commentaries. "Experience is necessary for the understanding of the Word. It is not merely to be repeated or known, but to be lived and felt." Luther's *sola scriptura* is inseparable from an interpretative practice meant to experience the Word's fulfillment, that is, the spiritual regeneration to which it refers. In this condition the *disposition* of the reader is crucial to allow scripture to emerge through interpretation, an interpretation that inevitably creates alteration of the established commentaries as well as the original text.

An alteration is also at the centre of Luther's translation of the Bible, which is not just the Word of God but also a way of gaining access to it, a way to proceed. Although before 1521 eighteen editions had appeared, they were not accessible to everyone. They were expensive, reproduced in a formal style, and translated from the Vulgate; Luther's was affordable and translated directly from the original Greek. But the goal was not to be philologically precise as much as direct and clear because Luther (echoing Erasmus' call for the Gospels and Epistles to be "translated into all languages,") wanted every town to "have its interpreter, and that this book alone, in all languages, would live in the hands, eyes, ears, and hearts of all people." In order to achieve this, as Michael Massing explained, "there was first of all the question of which German":

> Like the German lands as a whole, the German language was highly fragmented. There were two main variants: High German, spoken in the mountainous south, and Low German, spoken in the flat north. Within each group there were so many dialects that, as Luther observed, "people thirty miles apart can hardly understand each other. The Austrians and Bavarians do not understand the Thuringians and Saxons" ... Luther wanted a Bible that would speak to Germans of all regions and walks of life, from the magistrate at his bench

to the carpenter at his lathe, and so he needed to develop a new, more accessible idiom. To that end, he could draw on the rich lexicon he had accumulated on his long treks around Germany and from his encounters with the many layers of German society.[89]

Although this translation was also a way to contest the Church, which considered the Vulgate the only official Bible, Luther was much more interested in providing a *Volksbuch*, a people's book, accessible to everyone. This is why his translation into German is often free almost to the point of paraphrase. According to Dennis J. Schmidt, Luther did not simply stretch "the syntax, grammar, and vocabulary of German to be able to say what had been inexpressible in German prior to this translation" but also "united previously diverse linguistic groups."[90]

Luther relied heavily on Erasmus' edition of the New Testament (1519) to capture the sense and meaning of the biblical text, but he also developed a procedure that consisted in making a "a quick literal translation of the Vulgate Latin, using roughly the same word order. Then he would come up with synonyms for each word. Examining each phrase, he would consider the overall sound of the sentence, seeking a cadence that would make the words register and linger." As much as Luther wanted to produce a theologically correct Bible, he felt no hesitation in taking all the liberties translators inevitably take because it had to be rhetorically appealing to the German people. An interesting example is the Greek term *ekklesia*. While the Vulgate rendered it "*ecclesia*," or "church," Luther instead used "*Gemeinde*," meaning "community" or "congregation." "This reflected his view that the Christian community consists not of the institutional Church but of the body of all believers."[91] As we can see, Luther altered alien Latin terms – through his Christological hermeneutics – into folk German ones.

Published with a simple inscription, *Das Newe Testament Deutzsch* and the place of publication, within weeks all copies were sold and a new edition was planned. This was an opportunity for Luther not only to correct errors in the first edition but also to improve the confused orthography and purge the vocabulary of obscure words. From scholars and theologians to millers and blacksmiths, everyone was interested in his translation, which became the most bought German text "since the invention of the printing press seven decades earlier."[92] Luther's translation, his opposition to indulgences and the destruction inherent in his *sola scriptura* are the results of an alteration created through interpretation that forever changed the Bible, Christian faith, and the German language.

According to Heidegger, Luther, together with other writers from the Patristic period, was decisive in developing hermeneutics in a comprehensive and living manner through its "practical dimension." But the most important among them was not the famous translator of the Bible but rather Saint Augustine, who provided the first "'hermeneutics' in grand style." Afterward – in particular with Schleiermacher and Dilthey – hermeneutics was "reduced to an 'art [technique] of understanding' another's discourse, and seen as a discipline connected with grammar and rhetoric, it was brought into relation with dialectic – this methodology is formal, as 'general hermeneutics' (theory and technique of understanding any foreign discourse) it encompasses the special disciplines of theological and philological hermeneutics."[93] Against this "disastrous limitation" Heidegger praised the opening of book 3 of *On Christian Doctrine* (which Gegard Ebeling considered "historically the most influential work of hermeneutics"),[94] where the bishop of Hippo outlines how to approach the Bible.

> Man should approach the interpretation of ambiguous passages in Scripture with the following provisions: in fear of God, with the sole care of seeking God's will in Scripture; thoroughly educated in piety lest he should take pleasure in falling into quarrels over words; equipped with knowledge of languages lest he should get hung up on unfamiliar words and locutions; supplied with knowledge of certain natural objects and events which are introduced for purposes of illustration, lest he should misjudge the strength of their evidence; supported by the truth which the texts contain.[95]

Interpreting scripture for Augustine is a soul-searching and soul-shattering practice, to be undertaken in fear and trembling rather than with the certainty that every "technique of understanding" always involves. The alteration this practice puts in motion is not meant to find true and exclusive meaning but rather to allow its manifold readings to develop because there are several other routes to salvation besides the scriptures. These, even though they are human texts that refer to God, are not to be regarded in any sense as divine. This is why Augustine believed that a "person who bases his life firmly on faith, hope and love, thus needs the Scriptures only in order to teach others,"[96] in other words, it should not be obligatory reading. While "Augustine's interest in scripture as a controversialist and polemicist" is evident,[97] it also intertwines with the elaboration of a theory of knowledge whose goal is to introduce us into the inner word of the *voluntas*, or intention, of the *scriptor*.

Among the most important hermeneutic intuitions of the bishop of Hippo is that reading and interpretation are never universal or innocent. They always take place from a particular perspective that comes from the Bible. This is why interpreting scripture is not a purely epistemic process taking place between a subject and object but rather a fundamentally anxious mode of being that is continually striving for meaning. After all, as Augustine recalls in the *Confessions*, his first experience of scripture was to be repelled by them. But aren't we always anxious when we interpret obscure passages in texts? What should our disposition be when these passages emerge? Augustine's response to these questions discloses the anarchic vein of his hermeneutics, where the practical and living dimension of the Bible is opposed to its grammatical and literal features.

In contrast to the allegorizing tendencies of the Alexandrine school, Augustine begins with the premise that scripture is fundamentally clear, accessible even to children. In order to interpret scripture he recommends reading all the canonical books and acquiring familiarity with rhetoric as well as the Hebrew and Greek languages. When obscure passages emerge he suggests elucidating them by means of clearer ones but also with the help of other interpretations and translations. And Augustine insists that the spiritual disposition of the interpreter, especially *caritas*, as Grondin points out, is vital to interpretation of scripture as the most important manifestation of intentions.[98] But Augustine warns against readings that fail to search out the *voluntas*, or intention, of the *scriptor*, stopping short at his *scriptum* or *verba*. There is nothing more "appropriately called the death of the soul," he warns, "than that condition in which the thing which distinguishes us from beasts, which is the understanding, is subjected to the flesh in the pursuit of the letter (*sequendo litteram*)."[99] Augustine's hermeneutics, as Bruns points out, "implies a process in which one reinterprets oneself in order to enter into the conceptual scheme of another's inner intentions."[100]

Thus, any reading of scripture must be disciplined by a careful analysis of its language and grammatical structures in order to prevent the interpreter's becoming "a slave of signs." A slave worships a "significant thing without knowing what it signifies. But he who uses or venerates a useful sign divinely instituted whose signifying force he understands does not venerate what he sees and what passes away but rather that to which such things are to be referred."[101] The goal of Augustine's theory of signs – considered by many to be Augustine's greatest contribution to the development of hermeneutics – is to "limit the role of the Scripture, which he sees as human texts that refer to God but are not themselves to be regarded as in any sense divine."[102] In order to limit words' divine import, Augustine distinguishes between signs (*signa*) and signified (*significabilia*), between visual and auditory signs, and between signs that refer to other signs (such as "gesture" or "word") and those that refer to things (like "stone"). Words are *essentially* signs, but they are not *exclusively* signs because gestures, for example, are visual signs just as words are auditory signs. These distinctions are not meant to devalue language in contrast to reference but rather the *prophorikos*, outer word, in relation to the *endiathetos*, inner word, in which the revelations takes place. As Gadamer explained in *Truth and Method*:

The fact that the "*verbum*" is spoken differently in different languages, however, means only that it cannot reveal itself through the human tongue in its true being. In a depreciation of sensible appearance that is entirely Platonic, Augustine says, "We do not say a thing as it is but as it can be seen or heard by our senses." The "true" word, the *verbum cordis*, is completely independent of such an appearance. It is neither "*prolativum*" (brought forth) nor "*cogitativum tativum in similitudine soni*" (thought in the likeness of sound). Hence this inner word is the mirror and the image of the divine Word.[103]

But how can we communicate this "true" or "inner" word among us if it's not sensible? Original thinking and speaking are inner, a language of the heart; until they take on the form of a particular sensible or historical language, they remain for the most part purely intellectual and incommunicable. In dialogues, for example, we do not strive to understand the specific words or accidental form of the other's discourse but rather the *verbum* or reason that is embodied in it. The problem for Augustine is how to transcend the sensible, uttered language, in order to reach the true human word. If the *verbum*, like every merely human incarnation of the spirit, is never completely embodied, it's because it dwells within every language and is prior to all the signs into which it can be translated. "The doctrine of the '*verbum cordis*' warns us against taking the verbal sign to be ultimate. It always presents an imperfect translation ('*interpretatio*') that anticipates something more still to be said in order to comprehend the matter fully."[104] As we can see, there is a "processual element" in every attempt to find the word and the understanding that corresponds to it because the inner word precedes human utterance.

While Augustine acknowledges that the processual element could simply be a matter of misunderstanding, it is only *from within* that understanding can be guaranteed, that is, from the *verbum cordis*, because understanding presupposes conversion. "Nisi credideritis, non intelligitis": "Unless you believe, you will not understand."[105] So Augustine's hermeneutics is not meant to serve the doctrine of the Church but rather seeks the text in order to disclose the *voluntas* of the writer and the *verbum cordis*. While he discourages scriptural interpreters from reading carnally (*canaliter*, *corporaliter*), focusing only on the words instead of the intention behind them, he also warns against taking "alternate routes" (*traversa* and *perversa*) that can misinterpret the author's meaning in a particular text:

> In asserting rashly that which the author before him did not intend ("*non sensit*"), he may find many other passages which he cannot reconcile ("*contexere*") with his interpretation. If he acknowledges these to be true and certain, his first interpretation cannot be true, and under these conditions it happens, I know not why, that, loving his own interpretation, he begins to become angrier with the Scriptures than he is with himself.[106]

This description of the "errant interpreter's frustration" is important because it indicates how Augustine takes for granted not only authorial intention but also the hermeneutical expectation of the wholeness of scripture based on that intention. In this way, as Eden points out, he is describing the interpreter's "gradual reception of these individual passages as parts of a larger whole with the verb '*contexere*': to weave together ... To interpret Scripture, for Augustine, is in effect to weave its meaning."[107] The weaving or alteration that interpretation creates indicates that the obscurity of the scriptural texts is not a philosophical problem but rather a rhetorical issue meant to move the interpreter in her heart and mind.

The alteration that takes place when Augustine encourages all Christian interpreters to disclose the "intention of the writer" and the "true word" frees individual interpreters from slavery to signs but also enables reading the Bible spiritually, charitably, and equitably. While this interpretation implies a soul-searching and soul-shattering practice whose outcomes are uncertain, as we may say many things without having achieved ultimate clarity about them, it promotes *caritas*, which is the *summa* of all scriptural teachings. What "is read should be given careful consideration until an interpretation is produced that contributes to the reign of charity."¹⁰⁸ The fact there are several other routes to salvation beside the Bible (whose words' divine import has to be limited) reveals the anarchic vein in Augustine's hermeneutics: the priority of the practical and living dimension of the sacred word.

Luther's and Augustine's alterations of sacred texts were not meant to find the true meaning of the Bible, which is the goal of most biblical interpreters, but rather to set us free from its outer and inner restrictions. These, in the form of ecclesiastical establishments and grammatical signs, were perverting the Christian message. Even though Luther's opposition to the indulgences and his translation of the Bible can be considered a development of Augustine's theology of the inner self, they also disclose the anarchic vein of hermeneutics in its fullest. This vein has brought both thinkers to limit the role and meaning of the scripture in favour of its practical and intentional dimension. But the manifold readings and interpretations they recommended created an alteration that devalues the divine import of the sacred word and devalues those readers whose intentions and dispositions are doubtful. Luther's concern that he will not be judged worthy and Augustine's own conversion, which they narrate attentively, must be understood as calls for freedom that only hermeneutics could provide.

Part Three

Emergency

> Thinking politics exceptionally, however – through states of emergency or sublations of political subjectivity – blocks the representation of what is unintelligible or resistant to political theorization, while thinking politics unexceptionally spools into explanatory structures of historical epic and of classical political theory, muddying their structural coherence, obfuscating mainstream political and diplomatic ends.
>
> – Emily Apter, *Unexceptional Politics*

States of "exception" or "emergency" have become a central concept in contemporary philosophy after the terrorist attacks of 9/11 and the subsequent publication of *State of Exception* by Giorgio Agamben. The book was praised in the *New York Review of Books*, and, with two other thinkers that Agamben relies upon, Carl Schmitt and Walter Benjamin, it has become central to understanding and interpreting global politics after President George W. Bush's invasion of Iraq. The declaration of a state of exception, according to the Italian philosopher, has not only disclosed the performative expression of state power but also foreclosed any possibility of meaningful democratic politics. Almost twenty years later, another American president embodies the political predicament of our epoch. Donald Trump will not be remembered as the Texan politician is, for exercising extralegal powers to transform the "state of emergency" into routine political measures, but rather for denying pressing emergencies altogether. Trump incarnates a new condition where the greatest emergency has become the "absence of emergencies." Among the numerous emergencies that Trump conceals, climate change is certainly the most appalling, considering the ongoing consequences across the planet, but his indifference toward civil and human rights has also created outrage. But how must this shift – from "states of emergency" to "absence of emergency" – be interpreted? The problem is not only that the former "blocks the representation of what is unintelligible or resistant to political theorization," as Emily Apter recently suggested, but also its inability to respond to an ongoing global call to order and return to "realism," which Trump, together with other right-wing populists such as Marine Le Pen and Jair Bolsonaro, mobilizes as the defining political stance of current times.

The goal of this chapter is to understand this shift and to thrust us into three absent or hidden emergencies: the state of populist politics on the Left, global biodiversity loss, and the status and treatment of the revelations of whistleblowers. These are for the most part ignored at a global scale. But the absence of these emergencies is not simply the result of particular sovereign decisions but rather of our framed global order, which is a system of control over the emergence of emergencies into the sphere of popular and political action. This does not imply that the world is not full of emergencies that we hear of and watch government responses to every day: terrorist attacks, financial crises, and natural disasters are continuous emergencies. Rather, the greatest emergency today is that despite being the focus of mainstream news and popular alarm, these are still ignored, overlooked, or also discarded in terms of the arena of action. Before venturing into these absent emergencies it is necessary to recall Benjamin's, Schmitt's, and Agamben's takes on the "state of exception" or "emergency" as well as its most recent developments by Arne De Boever, Apter, Marie-Hélène Huet, Janet Roitman, Bonnie Honig, and Elaine Scarry. It is also necessary to differentiate this state from the new condition, which was first made clear by Martin Heidegger.

In order to understand the meaning of "exception" and "emergency" in the writing of these thinkers it's important to clarify first how the original German terms have been translated into

English. *Ausnahmezustand* and *Notlosigkeit* have repeatedly, although not exclusively, been translated as "state" or "lack" of "emergency." Whereas the first term is crucial in Schmitt's "state of exception" theory, the second has acquired substantial weight in Heidegger's writings after the turn to theorizing the "lack of emergency." After the publication of Agamben's text and Richard Polt's *The Emergency of Being*, *Ausnahmezustand* and *Notlosigkeit* have become synonymous for a number of contemporary philosophers, political theorists, and literary critics. But why choose "exception" rather than "emergency"? As Tracy B. Strong explains in his foreword to the English edition of Schmitt's *Political Theology* (translated by George Schwab) a dictionary will tell you that *Ausnahmezustand* means "state of emergency," but the idea of a "state of emergency" has "more of a legal connotation, and is more confined than an 'exception.'" The "exception is part of the 'order' even if that order is not precisely juridical."[1] The translation of *Notlosigkeit* for "distress" relies on similar arguments since in dictionaries this term has more of a psychological implication and is more restricted than "emergency." But how have these terms been translated so far?

Schwab rendered "Soverän ist, wer über den Ausnahmezustand entscheidet" as "Sovereign is he who decides on the exceptional case,"[2] and Harry Zorn, who translated Benjamin's "Theses on the Philosophy of History," translated "Die Tradition der Unterdrückten belehrt uns darüber, daß der 'Ausnahmezustand', in dem wir leben, die Regel ist" as "The tradition of the oppressed teaches us that the 'state of emergency' in which we live is not the exception but the rule."[3] Agamben has used the Italian equivalent of "state of exception," that is, "stato di eccezione."[4] Heidegger's "Woher die Notlosigkeit als die höchste Not?" is more complicated as the different translations demonstrate: "Whence the Lack of Distress as Utmost Distress?";[5] "Whence the lack of a sense of plight as the greatest plight?";[6] and it has been paraphrased as "How can the absence of emergency itself become an emergency?"[7]

As we can see, while the translators of Schmitt, Benjamin and Agamben used both "state of exception" and "state of emergency" to translate *Ausnahmezustand*, Heidegger's translators prefer "lack of distress," "lack of plight," and "absence of emergency" for *Notlosigkeit*. When a word is newly translated in a different form, is does not mean previous translators made a mistake but rather that it must be interpreted differently, an alteration to help overall comprehension. This alteration is at the centre of the difference between "exception" and "emergency" in relation to the problem of the sovereign, which is central in the particular uses of *Ausnahmezustand* in Schmitt, Benjamin, and Agamben. A similar alteration takes place with *Not* as "distress," "plight," and "emergency," which must be interpreted through Heidegger's *Notlosigkeit* in relation to Being's abandonment.

This brief discursion on the translations of *Ausnahmezustand* and *Notlosigkeit* was not meant to dispute which one is closer to the original German meaning but rather to point out how the popularity of the concept of "emergency" today is a result of both. However, this does not simply mean that *Ausnahmezustand* and *Notlosigkeit* are synonyms but rather that both refer to an emergency that concerns us at an existential level, that is, beyond theories of "the political." Although exceptionalism has become the *mot d'ordre* of a new century characterized by political states of exception, we are witnessing new critical interpretations in the work of contemporary political, social, and cultural theorists. But why, as we mention above, is the popular "state of emergency" (*Ausnahmezustand*) of Benjamin, Schmitt, and Agamben a consequence of Heidegger's "absence of emergency" (*Notlosigkeit*) and not the other way around? In order to respond to this question it is first necessary to briefly outline the problem of emergency in Benjamin, Schmitt, and Agamben.

The concept of emergency was a central issue of "Weimar thought," the thought developed between the First and Second World Wars, the Marxist secular Jew Benjamin and the archconservative Catholic Schmitt are at the forefront of this debate. Agamben, who relies on Samuel Weber's investigations, has shown that Schmitt's *Political Theology* is not only a response to Benjamin's "Critique of Violence" but part of a larger debate between the two thinkers that took place after 1925. The "exoteric dossier" of this debate is composed of the following documents:

Benjamin's citation of *Political Theology* in *The Origin of German Tragic Drama*; the curriculum vitae of 1928 and Benjamin's letter to Schmitt from December 1930 (both of which attest to an interest in and admiration ration for the "fascist public law theorist" ... and have always appeared scandalous); and Schmitt's citations of and references to Benjamin in his book *Hamlet or Hecuba*, written when the Jewish philosopher had been dead for sixteen years. This dossier was further enlarged with the publication in 1988 of the letters Schmitt wrote to Hansjörg Viesel in 1973, in which Schmitt states that his 1938 book on Hobbes had been conceived as a "response to Benjamin [that has] remained unnoticed."[8]

Agamben's goal is not only to widen the scope of Benjamin's thought beyond the conception of history but also to demonstrate how Schmitt's account of the sovereign decision on the exception corresponds to "the state of emergency in which we live" that Benjamin describes in *On the Concept of History*.[9] Agamben also shows that while "Benjamin concerns himself with a kind of violence that undermines the authority of the law ... Schmitt focuses on the decision that founds the law and constitutes the political authority of the sovereign. One could say that Benjamin is concerned with the end of the law, while Schmitt is concerned with its beginning."[10] The difference between these perspectives will clarify not only Schmitt's right-wing defence of the concept of sovereignty but also Benjamin's left-wing critique of that concept in relation to emergency.

Benjamin is renowned for having contrasted two conceptions of history with marked political implications: the continuous temporality of the humanist idea of cultural heritage and the disruptive constellation of the present and the past. The former is founded on a progressive flow of "homogeneous, empty time" directed to the future, but the latter is connected to all the failed causes and the struggles of those who lost their histories, which he calls the "tradition of the oppressed." A link with the problem of emergency takes place in the eighth thesis of *Thesis on the Philosophy of History* and *On the Concept of History* where

Benjamin declares that "the 'state of emergency' in which we live is not the exception but the rule." The German thinker's hope was that on the basis of this intuition "we shall clearly realize that it is our task to bring about a 'real' state of emergency" against the "fake" state of emergency in which the oppressed are living. The real state of emergency, that is, the abolition of dominion for a classless society, would "improve our position in the struggle against Fascism," allowing a revolutionary politics to "brush history against the grain," "blast open the continuum," and "leap into the past."[11]

In order to understand the implications of this radical politics it is necessary to recall how the tradition of the oppressed is related to the claim that there "is no document of civilization which is not at the same time a document of barbarism."[12] This statement is meant to contrast our "civilization," which is in part responsible for the "oppressed" condition of the weak, with "the angel of history" who wants to "make whole what has been smashed."[13] The greatest challenge for the angel is not only progress through the violent storm of events but also how it fosters the tradition of the oppressed, in other words, the "fake" state of emergency as a rule. This is why, for Benjamin, any revolutionary who fights for change should not be inspired by the image of a new order ahead but rather by the memory of the horror of the past. And it is why whoever emerges victorious participates

> in the triumphal procession in which the present rulers step over those who are lying prostrate. According to traditional practice, the spoils are carried along in the procession. They are called cultural treasures, and a historical materialist views them with cautious detachment. For without exception the cultural treasures he surveys have an origin which he cannot contemplate without horror. They owe their existence not only to the efforts of the great minds and talents who have created them, but also to the anonymous toil of their contemporaries. There is no document of civilization which is not at the same time a document of barbarism. And just as such a document is not free of barbarism, barbarism taints also

the manner in which it was transmitted from one owner to another. A historical materialist therefore dissociates himself from it as far as possible. He regards it as his task to brush history against the grain.[14]

Michael Löwy has pointed out how Benjamin's "real state of emergency" "is prefigured by all the revolts and uprisings that interrupt, if only for a brief moment, the triumphal procession of the powerful."[15] But the powerful always pretend to an authority and efficacy they do not really possess because they are unable to avert the state of emergency. Although Benjamin was influenced by Schmitt's admiration of the sovereign, he considers this concept unable to prevent the "catastrophic violence" of the state of emergency. If "the function of a tyrant," as Benjamin explains through examples from baroque tragedy in *The Origin of the German Tragic Drama*, "is the restoration of order in the state of emergency," then it is "a dictatorship whose utopian goal will always be to replace the unpredictability of historical accident with the iron constitution of the laws of nature," which is always doomed to fail. This is probably why he characterizes the sovereign as a "mad autocrat and symbol of a disordered creation" who, while making a hopeless "gesture of executive power," nonetheless reveals "at the first opportunity, that he is almost incapable of making a decision" that could avert the state of emergency.[16]

In order to avert this state of emergency Benjamin, in "Critique and Violence," attempts to justify the existence of a "divine," "pure," or "revolutionary" violence that lies beyond the sovereign and can break the ongoing dialectics between lawmaking violence and law-preserving violence. This divine violence creates a "real" state of emergency. Agamben, who pointed out how important this essay was for Schmitt, believes the strategy of the German jurist was to "lead such a violence back to a juridical context":

> The state of exception is the space in which he tries to capture Benjamin's idea of a pure violence and to inscribe anomie within the very body of the *nomos*. According to Schmitt, there cannot be a pure violence – that is, a violence absolutely

outside the law – because in the state of exception it is included in the law through its very exclusion. That is to say, the state of exception is the device by means of which Schmitt responds to Benjamin's affirmation of a wholly anomic human action ... For the distinction between lawmaking violence and law-preserving violence – which was Benjamin's target – corresponds to the letter to Schmitt's opposition; and it is in order to neutralize this new figure of a pure violence removed from the dialectic between constituent power and constituted power that Schmitt develops his theory of sovereignty.[17]

In order to understand Schmitt's theory of the sovereign and the state of exception (or "emergency") it must be pointed out how for him the Weimar Republic's economic hyperinflation, lack of political legitimacy, and constant threat from radical right- and left-wing groups was a symptom of a greater crisis: liberal modernity. In "The Age of Neutralizations and Depoliticizations" the German jurist explains how the dimension of the political has been neutralized by capitalism, technology, and atheism in order to deny modern societies a place of transcendence that was once provided by religion. The constitutional liberal state represented the embodiment not simply of this "depoliticization" but also of a mere administrative machine "without a transcendent or sacred dimension that would act as a point of legitimacy for public order. What was missing in the Weimar state was the 'spirit' of sovereignty, which was essential to any genuine political order."[18] As a political theologian, concerned with society's stable order, Schmitt saw in the progressive secularization of religious concepts an event of "disenchantment" that was effected by "liberal" economics and science. "The merchant sits in his office; the savant, in his study or laboratory. If they are really modern, both serve a factory – both are anonymous. It is senseless to claim they represent something."[19]

In this condition liberalism becomes "a consistent, comprehensive metaphysical system"[20] where a flattened-out world coincides with itself, leaving no space for the representation of a person that Schmitt considered essential to political legitimacy. In the European past the Catholic Church had filled this space through the person of God (Christ), or philosophers such as Hobbes had done so with an artificial persona (the Leviathan). Schmitt instead opts for the concept of the sovereign. This, as he explains, is a "borderline concept" that "is not a vague concept, but one pertaining to the outermost sphere. This definition of sovereignty must therefore be associated with a borderline case and not with routine." In order to restore transcendence, dignity, and legitimacy to politics, the sovereign must be understood from an *extremus necessitatis casus*, an extreme case of necessity, which is the exception. He is the only one authorized to make decisions in exceptional situations, that is, in states of emergency.

While the sovereign "is he who decides on the exception," and the exception is declared in the name of "public safety and order, '*le salut public*,' public well-being," what does the exception refer to? It is a situation in which the law temporarily suspends itself in order to enable the sovereign to maintain order and protect the law. But this is not a situation where the law is destroyed, one of "anarchy and chaos," but rather one in which the law recedes and order is maintained. While the German jurist explains how in these situations the sovereign power is revealed, he does not indicate the criteria he will use and leaves them to the sovereign's "competency." However, Schmitt does points out that it must be the same sovereign that "decides on the exception" as his decision also establishes a rule over what does not belong to the general norm of "ordinary legal prescription." The sovereign's decision on the state of exception is not of a kind with ordinary legal prescription because it includes something that is excluded from the normal operation of the law; in other words, it remains outside the law. Despite this, Schmitt insists that the decision concerning the exception is at the very foundation of the legal order because it decides whether or not the law applies.

Thus, the sovereign determines the most basic condition under which the law can function as only he decides "whether there is an extreme emergency," "what must be done about it," and "whether the constitution needs to be suspended in its entirety." But why must the exception have priority over the rule of law?

The exception can be more important to it than the rule, not because of a romantic irony for the paradox, but because the seriousness of an insight goes deeper than the clear generalizations inferred from what ordinarily repeats itself. The exception is more interesting than the rule. The rule proves nothing; the exception proves everything: It confirms not only the rule but also its existence, which derives only from the exception. In the exception the power of real life breaks through the crust of a mechanism that has become torpid by repetition.[21]

This mechanism is the liberal administrative state governed by norms and rules that Schmitt wants to overcome through the exceptional figure and power of the sovereign. If he does not present the sovereign simply as the authority outside the law but also as "a figure endowed with life who can act in the absence of rules," it is because "only an exceptional figure of this kind that has the capacity for general representation, who can provide a genuine point of transcendence and legitimacy, and whose absolute decision can unite and galvanize a social order."[22] While Schmitt guarantees that there is nothing that can truly depose the authority of the sovereign, he does recognize that the law includes the possibility of the sovereign's suspension in cases where the law cannot anticipate an emergency: after all, the "precise details of an emergency cannot be anticipated, nor can one spell out what may take place in such a case, especially when it is truly a matter of an extreme emergency and of how it is to be eliminated."[23] These cases include a violence that, while it undermines the law, also reasserts the most fundamental principle of the political–legal order, the sovereign's decision on the emergency.

Although Agamben's interpretation of legal violence and the exceptional state of modern politics relies heavily on Benjamin and Schmitt, he takes their intuitions a step further, reading them through Michel Foucault to show how the suspension of law has often been presented as a means of its preservation in modern political systems. This is evident in the states of emergency found in the American Civil War, in most countries involved in the First World War, in Weimar's social-democratic governments, and, more recently, during the presidencies of George W. Bush and Francoise Holland. All these governments made frequent use of the state of emergency and accustomed their citizenry to its limitations. The problem with "prolonged states of emergency," as Agamben explains, "in which police operations gradually replace judicial power, is that a rapid and irreversible degradation of public institutions must be expected."²⁴ In order to oppose these states of emergency – which are anything but shields for democracy – Agamben invites us to overcome traditional theories that still believe the state has to be suspended in the "exceptional" time of revolution in order to be restored afterward. Against these theories Agamben points out how the exceptional suspension of the rule of law happens so often now that we cannot treat the state as a solid, stable, and resistant concept anymore because "the state of exception … is included in the law through its very exclusion."²⁵

While Benjamin's interpretation of violence is vital to understanding the power of the sovereign – as it discloses the dialectic circularity between the violence that posits the law and the violence that preserves it – Agamben is dubious whether the divine violence can break this circularity. The problem is not only that Benjamin leaves the divine violence largely undefined but also the form it must take in order to confront the problems of modern sovereignty. Agamben also relies heavily on Schmitt to develop his theory of sovereign power but does not find the German jurist's notion of the *nomos*, the appropriation and division of land, the founding violence of the law as he claims. While he agrees with Schmitt's diagnosis that the order of the modern nation-state entered into a permanent crisis after World War I, he disagrees on its cause, finding instead a breakdown in the mechanisms through which life is framed by the law. Moving beyond Benjamin and Schmitt, Agamben suggests interpreting divine violence as what *entsetzt*, "de-poses," the law, and he seeks its origin in the appropriation and division of life through the sovereign's exception.

This relation among law, life, and the sovereign exception is at the centre of Agamben's *Homo Sacer* project, where he points out how the figure of the sovereign and *homo sacer*, "sacred man," can help break down the opposition between the normal legal structures and emergency powers that we have been accustomed to in the West. His goal is to demonstrate not only the ways in which politics and law are completely intertwined but also how the very idea of politics is about the possibility of the rule of law's becoming suspended in the sovereign's state of exception. The sovereign can suspend the law not because he is above the juridical order but rather because he is at the same time "outside and inside" this order, as Schmitt pointed out. Agamben calls this the "paradox of the sovereignty" because while the sovereign is the one who declares a state of emergency and can freely violate the letter of the law, his actions are legitimated by reference to the law whose goal is to restore its normal conditions. "The fact is that in both the right of resistance and the state of exception, what is ultimately at issue is the question of the juridical significance of a sphere of action that is itself extra-juridical."[26] But is sovereign action in the state of emergency, as Adam Kotsko suggests, not "a strange kind of legal illegality – or is it illegal legality?"[27] What takes place in the state of exception?

> What is at issue in the sovereign exception is not so much the control or neutralization of an excess as the creation and definition of the very space in which the juridico-political order can have validity. In this sense, the sovereign exception is the fundamental localization ("*Ortung*"), which does not limit itself to distinguishing what is inside from what is outside but instead traces a threshold (the state of exception) between the two, on the basis of which outside and inside, the normal situation and chaos, enter into those complex topological relations that make the validity of the juridical order possible.[28]

This space, which Agamben claims is the paradigm of modern politics, is the concentration or detention camp. Through the full manifestation of power over life this is where the "spatialisation of sovereign power" takes place as the detainee is turned into the *homo sacer*. This figure stands as a sort of metaphor for all people excluded from official legal protection and reduced to a state of *nuda vita*, "bare life," such as victims of concentration camp, enemy fighters, and refugees. By being locked out of the legal order these figures can be killed with impunity but not sacrificed; that is, "the killing of homo sacer is considered neither as homicide nor as sacrifice, since it is banished to a space that lies outside both human and divine law. Politics thus transforms into *biopolitics*: the political power over the bare lives of those sacred men, women, and children."29

Although this political power is thorough, Agamben points out a contradiction that overlaps in the sovereign's and the *homo sacer*'s respective relation to the law: "At the extreme limits of the order, the sovereign and homo sacer present two symmetrical figures that have the same structure and are correlative: the sovereign is the one with respect to whom all men are potentially '*homines sacri*,' and homo sacer is the one with respect to whom all men act as sovereigns."30 This paradoxical and contradictory relationship toward the law holds equally for the sovereign and victim, who are be images of each other.

The camp is not simply an event that marks modernity for Agamben but rather the *nomos* of the political space in which we still live and must continue to question. "Inasmuch as its inhabitants have been stripped of any political status and reduced completely to bare life, the camp is also the most absolute biopolitical space that has ever been realized – a space in which power confronts nothing other than pure biological life without any mediation."31

These camps, however, are not limited to those created by the Nazis in World War II and Camp Delta at Guantánamo Bay; the new refugee-detention centres in the European Union and Trump's America create the same space. Thus, we cannot interpret these camps only as extraterritorial spaces for individuals who have been banned from society but also as an essential component of the new geographies of terror meant to warn all of us, independently of whether we are inside or outside of the camp. When "the state of exception ... becomes the rule, then the juridico-political system transforms itself into a killing machine."32 Against this killing machine, Agamben suggests overcoming the destructive conjunction of sovereign authority and bare life even though it represents the deepest and truest structure of the law. This can only take place if the law is *entsetzt*, "de-posed," in other words, rendered inoperative.

"Agamben's greatest merit," as Bruno Gullì points out, "is that he has provided a clear philosophical focus, as well as a forum, for an understanding of the political and ontological structure of the suspension of the law." The philosophical insights of Benjamin and Schmitt are at the origin of the Agamben's hermeneutical operation, but President Bush's preemptive war had become the paradigmatic example of the new measure of global dominance, control, and detention. And the new aspect of the state of exception for the twenty-first century is that it no longer is a factor of the suspension of the law but rather no longer requires an emergency, in other words, the fact that it *could* arise is enough to suspend our freedoms. Agamben has shown how today it is not "the sovereign who decides of the state of exception ... but the other way around: the violence that posits the state of exception also decides on sovereignty, on who is the sovereign."[33] This is why with the progressive abolition of the distinctions among legislative power, executive power, and juridical power, contemporary theorist have begun to develop Agamben's intuitions in different directions: De Boever and Apter have weakened the sovereign and the ideological ambitions of the state of exception; Huet and Roitman suggest that emergency can also be interpreted through disasters and crises; and Honig and Scarry clarify how politics and thought can also take place through emergencies.

Although the presence of the sovereign and the state of exception are central in De Boever's and Apter's recent investigations, they do not hide the need to rethink these concepts to respond to new political challenges. De Boever goal is to "show that Agamben arguably does not fully abandon sovereignty in his thought but invites us to begin to think, instead, a plastic sovereignty." The notion of "plasticity," which he borrows from Catherine Malabou's interpretation of Hegel, is meant to continue "fluidifying solidified thinking," that is, to bring together the various kinds of life ("zoe," "bios," and bare life) that Agamben's ontology of sovereignty singles out. The three dimensions of plasticity that Malabou highlights – its ability to receive, give, and explode form – allow De Boever to pluralize sovereignty when it is paired with "plasticity." De Boever justifies this pairing:

> It seems that today, while the 9/11 window is closing and new political movements such as Occupy and the revolutions in the Arab world are on the rise ... the concept of sovereignty can and has played multiple roles in the analysis of both movements: as the target of Occupy's "horizontalism"; as the political power that could potentially keep the economic power; as a name for the popular organization against tyranny (abusive sovereignty) – as both an enemy and an ally. It thus seems that sovereignty, in spite of its claim to indivisibility, is in reality divided across a spectrum of concepts of the political and politics that nevertheless all have the value of organization, authorship, and accountability ... sovereignty's pluralization raises the bar for its critics, for one can no longer simply reject sovereignty wholesale and move on.[34]

The pluralization of sovereignty, when it is paired with "plasticity," allows De Boever to challenge the theologico–political nature of sovereignty. As many critics have pointed out, the binary distinction between "zoe" and "bios" is often exploited by tyrannical abuse, that is, to generate the explosive limit-form of life that Agamben calls "bare life." Plastic sovereignties permit the attuning of these abuses in favour of a "governmentality that would bring organization, rule, principle, accountability, authorship to the abyssal condition of human existence."[35] As we can see, De Boever's interest is not simply in a different defence of the figure of the sovereign but also to make sure it is adapted to respond to today's sociopolitical challenges.

Although Apter, in *Unexceptional Politics*, is also concerned with the return of the binary oppositions that sovereignties appeared to reinforce after 9/11, her goal is to resist through micropolitics the "state of exception" inscribed in theories of the political from Schmitt to Agamben. While these authors' ideological exceptionalism is unable to interpret what is incomprehensible and resilient to political investigations, the "routinization of the state of exception continues to underwrite drone warfare, supranational border patrol, domestic police practices, and the surveillance abuses of the National Security Agency; taken together they constitute an 'unexceptionalization' of illegal political intervention." Thinking unexceptionally, according to Apter, can counter the routinization of states of exception because it confronts us with the material and immaterial stuff of politics ("small 'p' politics") that operates behind the scenes. Micropolitics, as a form of unexceptional politics, discloses the events that alter, disturb, and interfere with the "politics that keeps the system of capitalo-parliamentarianism in place and prevents emancipatory politics from taking place."[36]

While De Boever and Apter alter the concept of the sovereign and the state of exception, Huet and Roitman invite us to broaden its origins and consequences through the concepts of disaster and crisis. These concepts allow them to illustrate a parallel between "the state of exception as suspension of the juridical order and the state of emergency brought on by disastrous events"[37] and to demonstrate how the term "crisis" has become "a blind spot in social science narrative constructions."[38] The goal of these authors is to show not only the role disasters and crisis can have within a state of emergency but also how its consequences are not restricted to the legal domain of political philosophy. This is why Huet believes:

> Our culture thinks through disasters. Implicitly or explicitly, disasters mediate philosophical inquiry and shape our creative imagination. The Enlightenment project is widely credited with the recognition that natural disasters were not sent by a wrathful God but stemmed from the workings of a violent universe. Plagues, earthquakes, and fire had to be understood – and exorcised – through the rational examination of physical causes. But the vision of a disaster willed by God was swiftly replaced by one of human-engineered calamity. If volcanoes erupted and the earth shook without divine intent,

humans made the damages greater and more grievous to bear. [The] state of emergency that characterizes current Western culture – which is related to what Agamben describes as a state of exception – stems from a pervasive anxiety about catastrophic events now freed from their theological meanings and worsened by human failures.³⁹

As we can see, Huet's interest is to show how the Enlightenment made natural disasters a properly human concern and set the stage for a sense of emergency that would condition our current political and legal responses. In order to outline this stage, the French scholar places a lot of emphasis on such catastrophic events as the 1755 Lisbon earthquake, which is commonly called the first modern disaster. It was among the first calamities to be interpreted through the lens of science and reason instead of a theological framework. But as Huet explains, the Enlightenment interpretation also bought a substantive blow to the idea of a purely natural disaster. With the growing sense of responsibility at stake in the managing of disasters it became clear that "there were no purely natural disasters, disasters wrought by physical disorders alone – only a combination of nature's fury and human negligence. All disasters involved problems of political administration."

According to Huet the denaturalization of the human soul not only disrupted the relations between the subject and the state but also guaranteed the imperfection of any political state. This imperfection is the result of the politicization of disaster, that is, the reassignment of the "natural disorder to the civil authority responsible for ensuring the well-being of citizens." This is why Agamben's examination of the history of the state of exception – as a gradual emancipation from the wartime situation to be used to expand government powers and suspend all legally established constitutional laws – cannot be interpreted as a creation of the democratic-revolutionary tradition rather than a natural or absolutist one.

Agamben holds that the state of exception was first defined by the French Constituent Assembly decree of 8 July 1791 (which envisioned the necessity for towns and ports in a state of siege to confer upon a single military command all the powers previously granted to civil governments), but Huet instead shows how it has been used every time a disaster struck and exceptional measures were applied to restore order. For example, "when it was rumored that the Regent had ordered the burning of the entire city of Marseilles during the 1720 plague, no decree and no vote was needed to confirm or dispel the rumor: absolutism itself allowed for the most extreme measures in times of emergency." Similar measures also applied under absolutist regimes because they required no official definition and no legal sanctions other than the sovereign's will. Thus, disasters represent the suspension of the natural order that discloses the mechanisms of nature's opening the "space for men's failure to control their costs and consequences."[40]

Although Roitman does not question Agamben's political philosophy, she believes there are good reasons to engage with his views as 9/11 "unleashed a great desire to examine and contest the consequences of a 'state of emergency' and a 'state of exception.' The invocation of crisis served to legitimate the abridgment of constitutional rights and the institutionalization of extra-juridical executive powers." The American anthropologist is not concerned with the sovereign's exceptional decisions as much as their epistemological consequences, that is, how the term "crisis" has now become the "noun-formation of contemporary historical narrative." The fact that crises no longer represent decisive events but are rather a state of being, a chronic condition we are continuously confronted with to the point that it becomes empty of its own content. Even though crises are proclaimed, they remain invisible as they are always reduced to other elements "such as capitalism, economy, neoliberalism, finance, politics, culture, subjectivity. In that sense, crisis is not a condition to be observed (loss of meaning, alienation, faulty knowledge); it is an observation that produces meaning." As political denunciations of particular situations that raise questions, crises open up pathways for action while closing others.

Roitman's examination of the 2007–08 bank bailout is a paradigmatic example of the production of meaning, knowledge, and narratives through crisis. Although the previous three decades saw massive deregulation of the financial system, giving markets more independence from the state, as soon as governments around the world saw the impact of a deep financial crisis, they took an unprecedented interventionist step: in order to guarantee financial institutions the state began to inject new capital into the markets. According to Roitman, the narrative of the crisis called for state intervention not as a possible response but as the only possible solution to the crisis. Thus, the problem of contemporary claims to crisis, which are often the grounds for the critique of capitalism, is that they are "not the grounds for alternative narratives or for other histories … The judgment of crisis is a distinction that produces information, which serves to reproduce existing dichotomies and extant hierarchies: public–private, economy–society, morality–politics, material–ideal, and so forth."[41] The fact that crises, as logical observations that generate meaning in a self-referential system, manage to reproduce these dichotomies is an indication that they also produce judgments of the validity of the institutions they seek to describe, which blocks any possibility of change.

While the four authors just discussed alter, examine, and develop Agamben's state of exception, Honig and Scarry instead want to show how politics and thought can also take place through emergencies. Suggesting that the state of emergency is the mark of a unitary political sovereign or the foreclosure of any possibility of meaningful democratic politics does not imply that there is no prospect of political resistance left. Honig and Scarry outline an "emergency politics" that can provide opportunities for democratic renewal and motivate citizens even in crisis. Honig, like Apter, wants to "de-exceptionalize" the sovereign and the exception in order to demonstrate that politico–legal decisions are products of human struggles and decisions rather than the simple application of preestablished rules:

> If we normally think of emergency politics as identified with a "decision" that puts a stop to ordinary life under the rule of law, then it might be useful to note that ordinary democratic

practices and institutions under the rule of law also feature "decision," those forms of human discretion presupposed by the rule of law but with which the rule of law is also ill at ease. In addition, if we think that sovereignty is sharpened and unified by emergency, we might also note that even the neo-Hobbesian, emergency-reproduced notion of sovereignty as unified and top-down itself has democratic qualities: It postulates popular subscription to sovereign power.[42]

Democratic politics for Honig is an agonistic activity that takes place beyond the singular event that theorists of exception focus on. While these confine politics only to the extraordinary frames of emergency and sovereignty, an agonistic theorist interprets them as part of ordinary political practices. This is why conflict, debate, and emergencies have a positive meaning for Honig. When contestation becomes a natural component of democratic society, emergencies can be interpreted as "contingent crystallizations of prior events and relationships in which many are deeply implicated." The goal of her political theory is not simply to democratize emergencies but also to interpret the sovereign's decision as an opportunity to confront these emergencies. The sovereign for her does not simply represent an executive power that must be chastened at all cost. Whereas those thinkers inspired by Agamben see a damning contradiction at the heart of sovereign power that ultimately leads to support of war, tyranny, and totalitarianism, an agonistic view sees the paradoxical relation between law and politics as generative of new possibilities.

In order to challenge the perceived notion that the state of exception leads inexorably to totalitarianism and war, Honig refers to the first Red Scare in 1919, when a series of coordinated bombings struck several US cities, which led the Justice Department to conduct raids and arrests. Anyone affiliated with communism, unionism, and anarchism was targeted, but foreign-born residents were the ones predominantly arrested and deported under the 1918 Sedition Act. While this was a classic case of a state of exception, as it urged an extralegal defence of the government, it also opened up a space to question powers within the government as an assistant secretary of the Labor Department, Louis Freeland Post, demonstrated at the time. He "defended the rights of the foreign born against those like Attorney General Palmer and J. Edgar Hoover ... who sought in wholesale deportations a solution to the anarchist threat and the problem of dissident action in the United States." Post, who was in charge of the deportation of those arrested by the raids, eschewed the expanded powers granted by the emergency to bypass normal judicial procedures and used the state of exception instead to expand the legal rights and protections of citizens to foreign-born residents.

Post's actions, as Honig points out, made it possible for the United States to survive the first Red Scare and "choose democracy over despotism."[43] This example shows how in a democracy it is possible to challenge the perceived notion that the state of exception leads inexorably to totalitarianism and also how the political dimensions of emergency cannot be reduced to its logic, that is, methods and procedures. The problem with this logic, which often requires fast acting, is how it is used to preclude the possibility of democracy in an emergency.

While Honig shows through the case of Post that the sovereign's decision is not the only outcome in a state of exception, Scarry instead is interested in reinvigorating the mechanisms of liberal democracies through the legal and political challenges the eight nuclear states (China, France, India, Israel, North Korea, Pakistan, Russia, the United Kingdom, and the United States) present today. The problem with our nuclear era is that it has not only normalized emergency but also "acted on the people of the world to make us surrender our powers of resistance and our elementary forms of political responsibility." In order to challenge this nuclear age, as well as other emergency situations, it is first necessary to overcome the prejudice of theorists of exception against thinking in emergencies. According to Scarry the prejudice comes from two sources:

> First, from a false opposition between thinking and acting; second, from a plausible (but in the end, false) opposition between thinking and rapid action. Now a third, equally

potent, form of seduction becomes visible: the acts of thinking that go on in emergencies are not recognized by us as acts of thinking. We misrecognize them. More precisely, we correctly recognize the presence of habit in these mental acts but incorrectly conclude that habit is incompatible with, or empty of, thought. We are therefore willing to set these mental acts aside. Our derisive attitude toward habit prevents us from seeing the form of thinking embedded in these cognitive acts and hence makes us willing to give up, or set aside, the most powerful mental tools that stand ready to assist us.[44]

In order to move beyond these false oppositions that often operate in emergency interventions Scarry invites us to interpret them pragmatically. This is why far "from being structureless, a crisis is an event in which structures inevitably take over. The only question is whether the structures will be negative or positive." Scarry does not seem to believe we are powerless to think and act democratically within emergencies because the emergency has a transformative dimension that not only transmits the state's interest in its population but also socializes people into democratic habits and attitudes. Preparing for an emergency – having fire drills, disseminating information for public review, and so on – socializes people into better democratic habits and attitudes. This is why in "an emergency, the habits of ordinary life may fall away, but other habits come into play, and determine whether the action performed is fatal or benign." While she believes we need to respond to emergencies with urgent action, this action must not preclude our thinking, which will ultimately judge whether the performed action was appropriate. If the task today is to live within a world of emergencies, then for Scarry the best possible way of doing so is to embrace procedures, deliberation, and democracy as cultural values that push us to work together to ensure our collective survival. Making sure these values "are widely understood – understood by the entire population – is one of the philosophic and civic responsibilities of our age."[45]

These six thinkers' interpretations and developments of Agamben's ideas on the state of exception highlight the significance of the sovereign's exceptional decision after 9/11 and indirectly refer to a condition that exceeds the realm of justice and politics.[46] The fact that "plastic sovereignty," "unexceptional politics," "disaster" as "culture" and a "blind spot for the production of knowledge," and "emergency" as a democratic renewal and motivation cannot easily be summarized under a single field of research is an indication that our existential condition seems to be the concern of all of these authors. As I discussed earlier, the translations of *Ausnahmezustand* and *Notlosigkeit* as "state of exception" or "emergency" and "absence of emergency" is the result not only of the popularity of "emergency" as a critical term but also of an existential emergency. The theorizing of emergency relates to the sovereign and the state of exception through emergencies, disasters, and crises, but the latter instead refers to Being's existential forgetfulness. The fact that this emergency, unlike the natural, financial, or humanitarian ones, seems out of date or theoretically irrelevant is an indication that it is crucial or, as Heidegger would say, the "greatest emergency." In order to understand why the popular "state of emergency" is a consequence of Heidegger's "absence of emergency," it is first necessary to understand the meaning of "emergency" for the German philosopher.

The concept of *Not* – "distress," "plight," or "emergency" – became central to Heidegger's thinking in 1930, when the technological replacement of Being with beings began to spread through all public and private realms of life. With this replacement, as I explained in chapter 1, the original meaning of existence as disclosure was lost and priority was given to beings as what factually exists here and now. Thus, fields of research such as politics, law, and anthropology are consequences of Being's forgetfulness, that is, of modern subjectivism, where an "object" is posited, identified, and applied to a "subject" independently of its meaning. Forgetting this meaning has not only devalued the thought of Being (existence) in favour of the technical use of beings but also transformed truth into a political, legal, and anthropological intuition. The problem with this intuition is that it is expressed through a correspondence between propositions and facts where the real is only what fits this correspondence, becomes calculable, and remains timeless. The world is reduced to objective measures, that is, realism.

Heidegger does not believe that politics, law, and anthropology are useless but simply that they are framed within this correspondence and without any possibility of change. In order to explain this condition it is useful to turn to the German term *Ge-Stell*, "framed" or "enframing," which Heidegger used to indicate the essence of technology. This word discloses the precise manner in which things or "reality" are held together and how we fit into this increasingly integrated system that today we generally call network. The problem now, as Heidegger pointed out, is that the "essence of man is framed, claimed and challenged by a power which manifests itself in the essence of technology, a power which man himself does not control."[47] Humanity does not control technology because we have become an integral part of its inevitable progress and success and also are in its service, that is, its servant.

As we can see, "framed" is a term that indicates the political nature of technology in this epoch of absent emergencies. Heidegger also called this the "age of the world picture" and the "machinational epoch" because the world has been reduced to a "predicable picture" where "machination" conceals Being. Humanity has established itself "as the measure of all measures with which whatever can count as certain" and also as "that being who gives to every being the measure and draws up the guidelines." These guidelines are meant to preserve everything predictable and calculable and to prevent any emergency:

> Human beings themselves, like the organized superman, seem to dominate everything and are dispropriated of the last possibility of their essence: they can never recognize in the extreme blindness that the human forgetfulness of being, a forgetfulness brought to maturity along with the abandonment of beings by being, leaves human beings without a sense of emergency insofar as it compels them to think that the ordering of beings and the instituting of order would bring about the substantive fullness of beings, whereas indeed what is assured everywhere is only the endlessly self-expanding emptiness of

devastation. The dispropriation of beings, which takes from them the truth of beyng, allows humanity, ensnared in such beings, to fall into a lack of a sense of emergency.[48]

As we can see, the problem for Heidegger is that we have lost touch with those tensions that animate history because our world has become one of technological objectivism, experiments, and relationships of function: "This is exactly what is so uncanny, that everything is functioning and that the functioning drives us more and more to even further functioning, and that technology tears men loose from the earth and uproots them."[49] In this condition man is only left with technical relations, which are framed within the progress of our global order.

After the first global economic crisis in 1929 Heidegger held a lecture course where he declared that this crisis and the oppression that accompanied it were not primarily an ontic issue but rather an existential one, that is, related to Being's forgetfulness. If these "economic, political, social, and cultural crises of the world depression in general and of the Weimar Republic in particular do not in and of themselves concern Heidegger," as Gregory Fried explains, it's because "these too are at most signs of Dasein's inability to take on the burden of Being. The search for reforms and solutions will only cover over completely the 'concealed' emergency."[50] But why is the word "emergency" always considered something evil or unfavourable? According to Heidegger,

> it is because we value freedom from emergency as a "good," and indeed we are correct to do so when at issue are well-being and prosperity. For these depend entirely on an unbroken supply of useful and enjoyable things, things already objectively present, ones which can be increased through progress. Progress has no future, however, because it merely takes things that already are and expedites them "further on their previous path."[51]

This unbroken supply of enjoyable things is responsible for concealing Being, that is, "what is genuinely to come and thus resides completely outside of the distinction between good and evil and withdraws itself from all calculation." But in order to value emergency outside this distinction, it is first necessary to "experience" the "emergency of the absence of a sense of emergency." For Heidegger this experience is the condition "where self-certainty has become unsurpassable, where everything is held to be calculable, and especially where it has been decided, with no previous questioning, who we are and what we are supposed to do."⁵²

While Heidegger's response points toward "the power that thoroughly dominates all technical production,"⁵³ – which we always served indirectly and today conditions most aspects of our existence – it is important to stress how its ability to frame emergencies is the greatest emergency. This does not mean that political crises such the treatment of refugees, government response to climate change, and the manipulation of elections by data-mining companies are not emergencies, but rather they are framed within our globalized framed order and emerge only as a consequence of this order. Within this order, where the future has become predictable through data mining and human genes can be altered through biogenetics, the problem is not only the emergencies we confront but most of all the ones we ignore, those that do not emerge from the background of ongoing crisis. It is important to remember that the verb "emerge" comes from Latin *e-*, "out of, forth, from, according to," and *mergere*, "to dip, plunge, immerse." When something emerges it takes part in a process of becoming visible after being forgotten, ignored, and concealed.

The problem with Agamben's "state of exception" or "emergency" (as demonstrated by the six critical interpretations examined in this chapter) is that it has become part of our globalized framed order. In this condition the foreclosure of any possibility of meaningful democratic politics is not the result of the sovereign's declaration of a state of emergency but rather of our global framed order, which is meant to maintain the absence of emergency. In order to awaken this absence one must distinguish not only between emergencies and absent emergencies but also between "those who rescue us from emergency" and those who "rescue us *into* emergency."⁵⁴ The tactics of the former are politics, law, and other disciplines that emerge from our framed order, but the latter instead thrust us into recognition of this order, which is now the greatest emergency.

According to Heidegger "this emergency must actually be experienced. What if humans are hardened against it, indeed, as it seems, more obdurately than ever? Then those who awaken must arrive, those who would be the last ones to believe they had discovered the emergency, because they are aware of suffering it." The thinkers who suffer the absence of emergency are the ones whose emergency is ultimately beyond the realms of politics, law, and other framed domains. This does not mean there are not emergencies related to these dominions but rather that they require a response that involves the larger global framed order, that is, the absence of emergency. When we are thrust into emergencies, we are exposed to the critical nature of matters such as the absence of left-wing populism, the global loss of biodiversity, and suppression of whistleblowers – and also to the possibility of freedom and salvation from the global framed order. If where danger grows, as Friedrich Hölderlin says, there is also the saving power, then "emergency does not first need help but instead must itself first become the help."⁵⁵ I will explore three political, environmental, and social emergencies within our framed global order to show how this thrust into emergency can offer the possibility of help.

EMERGENCY AND POPULISM

Although the rise of right-wing populism has been predicted for decades, little was done to confront it. While traditional centre-right and centre-left parties continue to espouse a neoliberal discourse that has run its course, leftists are afraid to endorse a populist stance because of the backlash from identity politics. Bernie Sanders in the United States, Jean-Luc Mélenchon in France, and Jeremy Corbyn in the UK have not managed to secure power, but right-wing parties have promoted charismatic candidates who now govern countries with a combined population of almost two billion people. The election of Jair Bolsonaro in Brazil is just the latest example of the resentment against the establishment that is now spreading throughout the world, demonstrated by the election of Rodrigo Duterte in the Philippines and Donald Trump in the United States. The number of Europeans voting for populist parties in national elections has risen from 7 percent to more than 20 percent since 1998; "one in four votes cast was for a populist party."⁵⁶ But the greatest emergency is not the rise of populism in different parts of the world but rather that only right-wing populists are viable to the point of winning elections, that is, the absence of left-wing populist alternative. In order to venture into this emergency it is first necessary to define populism and understand why so many people in the world's advanced democracies have turned to right-wing populist politicians within our global framed order.

The rise of populism in the twenty-first century will be remembered for how the difference between right-wing and leftist populism has been obscured. This distinction is vital, and overlooking it further contributes to the degradation of a public discourse that is already in trouble. When these differences are generalized, as Roger Cohen said, "populism" becomes a "catchall so broad that the only common thread it contains is the distaste for it felt by its facile users."⁵⁷ This rhetoric, to which the traditional political parties and the media outlets that have grown rich covering them are the main contributors, leads to a broader catchall, mobilization by rejection, a stance that harms democracy and cripples the possibility of change. Although the rise of populist politicians is the result of the long-term failure of neoliberal policies, it is also "a necessary dimension of democratic politics," as the political philosopher Chantal Mouffe said. "Instead of seeing the populist moment only as a threat to democracy, it is urgent to realize that it also offers the opportunity for its radicalization … It is only by restoring the agonistic character of democracy that it will be possible to mobilize affects and to create a collective will towards the deepening of the democratic ideals."⁵⁸ But to understand why so many people in the world's democracies have turned to populism, it is necessary to understand how harmful for traditional parties and voting habits throughout the West the moralization, technologization, and digitization of politics has been, which took place in the second part the twentieth century.

With the victory of the "free world" over communism, the universalization of liberal democracy, and the globalization of trade agreements, traditional parties began to believe partisan conflicts could be overcome through compromises. Democratic elections became all about establishing a discourse beyond "sovereignty" and "opposition," "left" and "right." But aren't these necessary components of a healthy democratic society? Societal debates arise not simply because we are conflictual beings with diverse values, traditions, and beliefs but also because we are suspicious of the possibility of universal rational compromises. The problem with these compromises, as we are now experiencing in the European Union, is that the deliberations they embody are always framed; that is, they do not involve real choices among alternatives.

Timothy Giddens's "third-way" political theory in the 1990s was among the first to represent this modern frame, as its implementation through Tony Blair's New Labour policies demonstrated. The British scholar explained that the goal of his idea was to create "a one-nation politics" where "no authority" could take place "without democracy." This is framed democracy, where the submission of laws to the "consensus at the centre" is the only democratic, that is, acceptable outcome of politics. This framing claimed that it overcame traditional oppositional politics, but instead it substituted moral categories – "good" and "evil," "right" and "wrong" – for the language of competing political ideas, giving rise to a moralization of politics. As the third way embraced neoliberalism and hid the language of debate behind curtains of political correctness, it not only obstructed democratic channels of expression for diverse political stances but also delegitimized them. This moralizing vocabulary, together with the third-way imperative of bipartisan consensus, has led to further shrinking of the difference between the parties of the left and the right and, as choices disappeared, a withering popular interest in politics:

By claiming that the adversarial model of politics and the left/right opposition had become obsolete, and by celebrating the "consensus at the centre" between centre-right and centre-left, the so-called "radical centre" promoted a technocratic form of politics according to which politics was not a partisan confrontation but the neutral management of public affairs. As Blair used to say: "The choice is not between a left-wing economic policy and a right-wing one but between a good economic policy and a bad one." Neoliberal globalization was seen as a fate that we had to accept, and political questions were reduced to mere technical issues to be dealt with by experts. No space was left for the citizens to have a real choice between different political projects and their role was limited to approving the "rational" policies elaborated by those experts.[59]

While Giddens and Blair presented this "postpolitical" situation as progress for democracy, it was in fact the beginning of a process of disaffection with democratic institutions manifested in the increasing level of abstention at elections. If democracy wants to preserve its superiority among other political systems, as Ernesto Laclau and Mouffe suggest, it must return to the people. And this is what populism does. It is "a way of constructing the political on the basis of interpellating the underdog to mobilize against the existing status quo."[60] It brings together different demands in opposition to a common enemy. Contrary to other political analysts, such as Cas Mudde or Jan-Werner Müller, Laclau and Mouffe do not consider populism an ideology but rather a political form capable of articulating identities, interests, and needs that have been delegitimized by the centre-right and centre-left parties. Moreover, they do not believe that this strategy as it is applied by populist politicians is designed exclusively to obtain power; it is also a necessary effort to overcome the lack of alternatives embodied by the traditional parties of the past decades against the status quo. This can be done from the most diverse ideologies and involves, as a result, a far wider ensemble of differences.

As a consequence of framed democracies, populism has become the only productive form to take into account the demands of the people and to promote collective participation. But just as there was once a substantial difference between right- and left-wing policies, there is also a difference between rightist and leftist populism. Although both apply the same principle – bringing together a crowd around a political idea in order to shape an "us" against a "them" – the concepts used to define these groups are radically different. This is evident in the emotions each side uses to mobilize voters: fear of the foreigner on the right and hope for a better future on the left. The former is rooted in hatred and indifference, and the latter, in justice and equality. This strategy was evident in Trump's and Farage's campaigns, where they restricted the national identity of "the people," excluding immigrants, refugees, and any Other definable as "foreign" to a sentimental ideal. Instead of excluding categories of people, Sanders and Corbyn focused on those sectors of the establishment at the service of neoliberal global corporations. For the former, this meant "breaking up the big banks" and, for the latter, "strengthening workers' rights." In sum, the concealed emergency of populist politics is not the emergence of right-wing populism but rather the absence of leftist populism capable of opposing its hatred and indifference.

This hatred and indifference is particularly marked in Trump, who has become the paradigm of the right-wing populist politician. His election in 2016 illustrates the failure of the centrist "left" Democratic Party to endorse a populist leftist candidate (Sanders) and also its inability to predict Trump's rise to power despite the warnings of intellectuals. The most notorious example is Richard Rorty.

In 1998 the great American philosopher released *Achieving Our Country: Leftist Thought in Twentieth-Century America*, where he warned that members of the labour unions and unorganized unskilled workers would "sooner or later realize that their government is not even trying to prevent wages from sinking or to prevent jobs from being exported." While suburban white-collar workers, also afraid of being downsized, "are not going to let themselves be taxed to provide social benefits for anyone else," the "nonsuburban electorate will decide that the system has failed and start looking around for a strongman to vote for – someone willing to assure them that, once he is elected, the smug bureaucrats, tricky lawyers, overpaid bond salesmen, and postmodernist professors will no longer be calling the shots." But Rorty predicted a strong man not only with these characteristics but also with a plan similar to Trump's:

> One thing that is very likely to happen is that the gains made in the past 40 years by black and brown Americans, and by homosexuals, will be wiped out. Jocular contempt for women will come back into fashion. The words "nigger" and "kike" will once again be heard in the workplace. All the sadism which the academic Left has tried to make unacceptable to its students will come flooding back. All the resentment which badly educated Americans feel about having their manners dictated to them by college graduates will find an outlet.[61]

This "outlet" was going to be a consequence of Democrats' giving "cultural politics preference over real politics." While Rorty's prediction today sounds prophetic, it received a critical reception when his book was released. This was probably cause for his scepticism towards the Democrats' willingness to resist neoliberal forces favouring corporate globalization and deindustrialization. This inability led Democrats, as Nancy Fraser recently pointed out, to create a new hegemonic bloc: progressive neoliberalism. Progressive neoliberalism is an "alliance of mainstream currents of new social movements (feminism, antiracism, multiculturalism, and LGBTQ rights), on the one side, and high-end 'symbolic' and service-based business sectors (Wall Street, Silicon Valley, and Hollywood), on the other." In this alliance, boosted during Bill Clinton's tenure, progressive forces were merged with forces of cognitive capitalism, especially financialization, and ideals like diversity and empowerment began to serve "policies that have devastated manufacturing and what were once middle-class lives." In this way, Democrats not only ignored the increasing social inequality that affected most citizens but also draped "their project in a new cosmopolitan ethos, centered on diversity, women's empowerment, and LGBTQ rights."[62]

To a certain extent, Barack Obama and Hillary Clinton embody Rorty's characterization of "cultural politics" and Fraser's *progressive* neoliberalism, which lacks a leftist economic agenda; they ignored the declining economic condition of American workers that was a consequence of the globalization they lauded. With no political voice speaking to or on behalf of the concerns of labour, workers turned against the technocratic policies of the cultural elite and either opted out of politics or followed the demagoguery of Trump's right-wing populism. The problem now is not that economic globalization is being rejected but that it is repudiated with the cosmopolitanism that accompanied it. This rejection has quickly turned into anger and resentment at all the politicians, intellectuals, and elites who overlooked social inequality, as economists such as Joseph Stiglitz and Thomas Piketty have been pointing out. In sum, Trump's victory was not solely a revolt against "neoliberalism tout court, but *progressive* neoliberalism."

As we can see, the emergency today goes deeper than the victory of Trump's right-wing populism, though the xenophobic nature of his government is profoundly troubling. But the failure of left-wing populism constitutes the greatest emergency of democracy. Sanders did not manage to win the party primary contests, an exercise in corporate governance designed to defang populist ideas, and his party continues to favour bipartisan candidates. Yet it is right-wing populism, now elected to positions of power, that is not compatible with a pluralist conception of democracy in the twenty-first century. The left-wing populism of Sanders, Corbyn, and Mélenchon represents the only chance that the parties of the framed democracies have to defeat the right-wing populist monster they have unleashed.

EMERGENCY AND BIODIVERSITY

The absent emergencies of our current condition are hidden behind the rhetoric of crisis. Even those emergencies that are discussed in public and reported in mainstream sources are co-opted and hidden by the very discourse that purports to disclose them. In this way, the very act of announcing an emergency participates in its absence as the announcement becomes subject to the dominant framed discourse. Adrian Parr, who also draws upon the work of Agamben, Honig, and Scarry, believes this process is expressed in contemporary environmental emergencies. This is why the truth about them is never exposed by any "representation ... that translates the situation into a security issue, or the spectacular images of devastation and death flooding the media, or even the alarming statistics reported by international and nongovernmental agencies. Truth is revealed where there is no representation, from where representations are produced – in other words, in this instance where the state of exception is legitimated." Although these legitimations occur every time governments deny the scientific evidence of climate change, withdraw from international agreements, or exercise emergency powers to place activists under surveillance, environmental emergencies ultimately lie "beyond the rule of law."[63]

In order to understand how environmental emergencies are rendered absent within our global framed order, it is not enough to stress how their devastating effects are concealed by corporate media, executive power, or law enforcement because the numerous temporalities of climate change also play a central part. The effects of climate change are gradual; that is, they extend through time. Although natural disasters can take place abruptly, few have the sociopolitical impact of terrorist attacks or social riots. For example, while the French government of Emanuel Macron can ignore the 48,000 yearly deaths across France caused by air pollution, it cannot disregard the death of ten civilians during the "yellow vest protest" at the end of 2018. Whereas the latter is treated as an emergency in the literal sense – an emerging event that must be confronted instantly with the full power of the law – the former is made an absent emergency, a symptom of our condition that ultimately is more dangerous. The other obvious difference, of course, is that the government can use the protest to bolster its own power rather than the admission of ineffective and negligent policies betokened by the much greater number of deaths that take place over a longer time. The different temporalities of environmental degradation allow more opportunities for the stabilization of the global framed order. *Parr summarizes the problem:*

> The pressing problem all life on earth is facing with climate change is less spatial than it is temporal. In other words, there are numerous temporalities to the emergencies posed by environmental degradation. First, there are short-term extremities, such as those that arise when natural disaster hits. Then, there is the nonteleological and prolonged steady state of ecological forces activating multiple affects, forming new connections with energetic systems (waves, El Niño, melting ice caps) and destabilizing the fragile equilibrium balancing life on earth, pushing it to the tipping point. These work in conjunction with the forces of globalization, capital accumulation, and militarism conjugating and provisionally stabilizing one another.[64]

The result of this stabilization is a condition where environmental emergencies are absent, subject to the global order's dominant discourse. This is particularly manifest in the climate-change-driven loss of biodiversity, which, because it is gradual and can be hidden with the passage of time, Cristiana Pașca Palmer, the UN's biodiversity chief, calls "a silent killer." Unlike other related environmental emergencies, such as wildfires and hurricanes, that are obvious and sudden symptoms of climate change, biodiversity loss is a "nonteleological and prolonged" ecological degradation where the "forces of globalization, capital accumulation, and militarisms" can easily operate. This operation is visible in their inequitable effects upon the interactions of diverse species that determine the fundamental characteristics of our ecosystem.

In order to understand these effects it is important to recall that biodiversity constitutes one of Johan Rockström's nine planetary boundaries within which humans can continue to live sustainable lives. Biodiversity, also referred to as "biosphere integrity," is one of the four already transgressed. The other three are "climate change" (rising levels of greenhouse gases in the atmosphere), "deforestation" ("land-system change"), and "biogeochemical flows" (phosphorus and nitrogen cycles). With climate change, biodiversity is considered a "core boundary" because its loss can lead to a deterioration of human well being throughout the world. Defined as "the variety of life on Earth – its genes, species, populations, and ecosystems," biodiversity contributes to the regulation of the stability of ecosystems. The "functioning of an ecosystem is critically dependent on the biodiversity of its constituent species and populations, and it is this functioning that determines the ability of ecosystems to provide the essential goods and services that keep humans and all other species on the planet alive."[65]

As I have said, the problem of this fundamental core contributor to regulating the state of the planet is that unlike other human-made effects of climate change that can be seen in everyday life, it is nonteleological, gradual, and silent. We are generally unaware that human activity takes up as much as 50 percent of all the photosynthesis on the planet, claiming the basic food supply. The number of animals living on Earth has plunged by half since 1970. Just "tiger numbers have plunged by 97% in the last century."[66] The loss of plant and sea life will reduce the Earth's ability to absorb carbon from the atmosphere, creating a vicious cycle that can be halted only if we find a new way to think about economies. We need to take more account of the future costs of the luxuries we take today, when our current economic indicators (such as GDP) have become counterproductive.

While biodiversity loss has not reached a point of no return, it has already pushed the planet into a new state, hostile to our own survival, with massively insufficient supplies of food, water, and energy in different parts of the world – though generally less so in the framed democracies of the West. Though the goal of the 2018 United Nations Biodiversity Conference in Egypt was to begin frenetic negotiations toward an ambitious new global deal at the next conference in Beijing in 2020, the possibility of action is constrained because these negotiations are conducted by the capitalist and framed institutions that sponsor and attend them. Thus, the greatest emergency is not whether this deal will be reached but rather how an emergency that threatens to make humanity "the first species to document [its] own extinction"[67] is still silent, absent, concealed by the discourse of the very groups that claim to combat it on our behalf.

Thus, the loss of biodiversity from climate change or, more accurately, from the political refusal to engage the existential nature of climate change is another hidden, absent emergency within our framed global order. Even before right-wing populists came to power, climate change was both ignored and contested by governments despite the efforts of the scientific community to warn us over the past decades. As Marco Lambertini said, we are now about to reach a point of no return, with a 60 percent loss of biodiversity since 1970.[68] This point of no return in a changing climate coincides with the sociopolitical awareness that to speak of environmentalism under neoliberal democracy has become futile.

Almost thirty years after the creation of the annual Intergovernmental Panel on Climate Change and the United Nations Conference on Environment and Development, also known as the Earth Summit in Rio, CO_2 emissions, continue to increase (rising 1.4 percent in 2017), mainly because of coal burned for electricity. This increase is not caused by scientists' inability to demonstrate the effects of CO_2 emissions but rather by our globalized framed order. This is why the question now is "not so much if but by how much and how quickly the climate will change as a result of human interference, whether this change will be smooth or bumpy and whether it will lead to dangerous anthropogenic interference with the climate."[69]

Within this order, climate conferences and summits are meant to fail. A paradigmatic example of this failure was the agreement reached at the Copenhagen IPCC summit in 2009, when the United States and China agreed to keep temperatures from increasing more than two degrees Celsius. This agreement was not made for the environmental balance but rather to allow trade agreements (NAFTA) and organizations (WTO) to increase the deregulation of capital at a global scale. Only once since 1988 – the year that marked the beginning globalization as we know it – have global carbon emissions risen at less than a 3.4 percent annual increase, and the cause of this interruption was not the IPCC or some other climate agreement but the world financial crisis of 2008–09.

Indeed, when the latest environmental degradation erupts, world leaders respond not by seeking root causes or acknowledging the absent emergency but instead instituting a state of emergency, which has become the engine of liberal democracies. But there are not many states of emergencies left to announce, considering the 2019 Intergovernmental Panel on Climate Change stated we "only have 12 years left to pull the planet back from the brink of climate emergency."[70]

EMERGENCY AND REVELATIONS

The revelations of whistleblowers have received substantially more attention in the media these past decades than biodiversity loss. When Julian Assange revealed (through the Chelsea Manning leak) how coalition forces in Afghanistan killed hundreds of civilians in unreported incidents and Edward Snowden revealed that the NSA was operating a secret surveillance program, every media outlet in the world reported their revelations. The problem with these revelations is not the justified attention they received but rather how little change it generated and how it was followed by the detainment of the whistleblowers. While the war in Afghanistan continued and the NSA was barely reformed, Assange was recently arrested by the UK authorities after being confined within the embassy of Ecuador in London for seven years, Snowden lives in Russia after being granted asylum, and Chelsea Manning after being imprisoned for seven years was jailed in 2019 for her refusal to cooperate with a grand jury investigation into WikiLeaks. What this pattern reveals is how challenging and dangerous it is to disclose revelations – to attempt to thrust us *into* emergency – within our global framed order. In this condition the greatest emergency is not what the whistleblowers reveal but rather the forces at the national and international levels that are brought to bear to prevent these revelations from thrusting us into emergency and disclosing the nature of its imposed absence. These forces stand between revelation and change. This is particularly meaningful in Christopher Wylie's revelations concerning Cambridge Analytica's involvement in Brexit and the Trump 2016 campaign given the central role that Facebook played. In order to venture into this revelation and its absent consequences, it is first necessary to understand what sort of political subjects whistleblowers are.

The disclosures of whistleblowers are the paradigmatic example of how framed our global order has become. This is probably what drove Assange, Manning, and Snowden (and other less well known whistleblowers such as Sherron Watkins, Coleen Rowley, and Antoine Deltour) to risk their lives in the first place. When the level of state secrets and mass surveillance begins to invade our civil liberties and privacy, it becomes necessary to take a stand. This is why Snowden, Assange, and Manning, as Geoffroy de Lagasnerie explains, should not simply be seen as "whistleblowers" whose activities involved the diffusion of confidential information but rather as bringing a "new political art" into existence where resistance takes a different meaning. "It is not simply a matter of new points of dissent arising and coming to occupy the public spotlight. Rather, what we are seeing are new modes of subjectification" that "promote the emergence of subjectivities emancipated from prescribed and established forms of politics." Although Assange, Manning, and Snowden practised and encouraged different forms of resistance, according de Lagasnerie, a common *technē* unifies them.

> It is a matter of renewing – and perhaps radicalizing – the call for democracy in the Internet age. Snowden, Assange, and Manning are reactivating the political and legal struggles against arbitrary state power that have been playing out since the nineteenth century. The questions they pose about private life and surveillance, illegal acts committed by authorities, and state secrets are fed by a democratic ambition. The point is, on the one hand, to protect the personal realm against state intrusion and, on the other, to extend the supervision exercised by the ruled over those who rule – in defiance of the fact that

the political field increasingly has come to operate in secret, by taking the liberty to make decisions hidden from citizens.[71]

The revelations of whistleblowers are invitations to rethink our understanding and practice of democracy. This is why Assange characterized himself as the "spy of and for the people" and Snowden, as another citizen committed "to greater transparency." Their goal is not simply to inform through revelations but also to involve us in monitoring the decisions of governments and corporations regarding our freedoms. Whistleblowers, as Slavoj Žižek points out, "render public the unfreedom that underlies the very situation in which we experience ourselves as free."[72] The alliance of state security agencies and data-processing companies like Google or Facebook is meant to secretly manipulate our allegedly free choices. Although formal freedoms are officially guaranteed within our framed global order, the truth is that most of the time even fully enfranchised citizens are not aware of the extent to which we are controlled and manipulated within this order. This awareness is at the centre of Wylie's revelations of Cambridge Analytica's operations.

Cambridge Analytica was a data analytics firm created by the former White House senior strategist Steve Bannon, the SCL Group political and defence contractor Alexander Nix, and Wylie, a data scientist. Robert Mercer, a hedge fund billionaire, Trump supporter, and former AI engineer, invested $15 million in the firm after being assured it could identify the personalities of American voters and influence their behaviour. The firm, as Wylie revealed, was meant to build Bannon "an arsenal of weapons to fight a culture war" as he believed that "politics is downstream from culture." Cambridge Analytica was testing messages such as "drain the swamp" and "build the wall" before the Trump campaign existed, and one of the things that provoked Wylie to reveal the firm's operations was Bannon's interest in "voter disengagement and the idea of targeting African Americans."[73] These, for example, were reminded of Hillary Clinton's 1990s description of black youths as "super predators" in the hope that it would deter them from voting.

In order to achieve this, Wylie, who oversaw the operation, assembled a team of psychologists, data scientists, and academics to develop a new targeting technology for political ads. The greatest challenge they faced was obtaining vast amounts of voter data. As Wylie revealed, this became possible in particular through Aleksandr Kogan, the Russian American Cambridge University researcher who obtained permission from Facebook to run a personality quiz on their social network. The quiz was taken by 270,000 users on his app "thisismydigitallife," apparently for academic purposes. Users were paid by Cambridge Analytica to take the quiz, and their participation granted the app access to their friends' profiles. This enabled Kogan's app to collect data from approximately 87 million users without their consent.

Wylie, who worked with Kogan to obtain and process the data for Cambridge Analytica, said they "exploited Facebook to harvest millions of people's profiles. And built models to exploit what we knew about them and target their inner demons. That was the basis the entire company was built on." This data became vital for Wylie's algorithms, which analyzed different personality traits (from sexual orientation to fashion preferences and religious affiliation) and created sophisticated psychological and political profiles. These profiles were later targeted by political ads designed to manipulate their particular psychological makeup in favour of the Leave campaign during the Brexit referendum and play a key tool in digital operations during Trump's election campaign.[74]

Wylie, according to Carole Cadwalladr, was particularly driven to reveal the details of the operation when he became aware the firm's parent company (SCL) had won contracts with the US State Department and begun pitching to the Pentagon. He could not believe that after the "company has created psychological profiles of 230 million Americans ... they want to work with the Pentagon? It's like Nixon on steroids." This alliance between private data-processing companies and state security agencies to deploy behavioural technologies, together with Nix's denial of using Facebook data during a public hearing of the British House of Commons' parliamentary committee investigating Cambridge

Analytica, drove Wylie to disclose what seems today to be "the end of the age of data innocence."⁷⁵

Like the revelations of Assange, Manning, and Snowden, Wylie's shows how framed and manipulated we are within our global order even when we vote democratically. Cambridge Analytica's use of Facebook information and internet history to influence elections is secondary to the revelation of how the social media was designed to function. The experience of freedom generated by Facebook, and by the internet in general, must be interpreted as the progressive digitalization of our lives for purposes we are unaware of. As the internal e-mails obtained by the House of Commons Digital, Culture, Media and Sport committee at the end of 2018 show, as far back as 2012 Facebook's worry was not about data misuse but rather how to use developers' apps to encourage its own growth.⁷⁶ Cambridge Analytica was just another client, always meant to exploit intimate details about the private lives of millions for profit, and we should expect similar scandals in the future because almost nothing has changed since Wylie's revelations.

Despite the many federal, congressional, and parliamentary commissions throughout the democratic West investigating the role of Cambridge Analytica and Facebook, "there haven't been any consequences." "My journey as a whistleblower," Wylie says, "has also been a journey in understanding institutional failure." Although Cambridge Analytica shut down and Facebook was fined US$645,000 by the UK Information Commissioner, only Wylie, Nik, Kogan, and Mark Zuckerberg have been called to testify by different commissions. The fact that Mercer and Bannon still haven't been called is an indication that the interference in democratic referendums and elections does not constitute an emergency today. Wylie's revelations demonstrate not only that individuals are much more easily controlled and manipulated when they continue to experience themselves as free and autonomous agents but also how little change takes place when this manipulation is revealed.

Afterword

> Constantly bombarded by so-called "free choices," forced to make decisions for which we are mostly not even properly qualified (or about which we possess inadequate information), increasingly we experience our freedom as what it effectively is: a burden that deprives us of the true choice of change.
> — Slavoj Žižek, *Like a Thief in Broad Daylight*

Society is supposed to be the realm within which citizens can practise their rights, artists present their creations, scientists make their discoveries, and intellectuals interpret whether all of these are freely done. But "society" can also refer to a civilization's current political and cultural condition. This is why one of the most alarming consequences of the absence of emergency generated through the intensification of control and return to order is the decline of freedom – as if history, society, and culture have ended. But have they? Even though such terms as the "age of anger," the "network society," and the "culture of fear" seem like simple journalistic slogans to describe our condition, we must continue to seek different interpretations of our age because they help us respond properly to its challenges. When Pankaj Mishra, Manuel Castells, and Barry Glassner coined these terms they were trying not simply to establish once and for all the conditions under which we live but rather to invite us to understand the current form of our world and to take an existential stand.

Philosophers often respond to the question of how we ought to live by declaring the end of epochs or concepts. Francis Fukuyama declared the end of history; Arthur Danto, that of art; and Slavoj Žižek, that of nature. Perhaps we should also declare the end of freedom, considering the level of global control and technological manipulation we've reached. Now that social media are also used to spy on society and manipulate electoral processes, freedom cannot be understood anymore as a property of the subject, an intersubjective activity, or even as a guarantee of liberal democracies. Rather, it is an interpretative practice that strives to continue at large. "Interpretation," as Gerald Bruns says, "has always tried to go beyond itself, that is, to free itself from its accumulated history and to lose itself, in some fashion, in whatever there is to be understood."[1]

As we've seen in this book, interpretation is not a contemplative, calm, and disengaged activity; it is an active practice that requires an anarchic effort. This effort is directed against those who call for alternative facts, that is, the return to realism that drives our global framed order. While those who submit to this order describe the world in order to preserve it as it is, the others interpret to disrupt and change it. The goal of philosophers today is no longer to disclose origins or differences but rather to interpret alterations, disruptions, and emergencies, in particular when they are absent. This is why freedom, within the call to order that pervades the so-called ongoing return to reality, facts, and truth in the twentieth-first century, becomes a "burden that deprives us of the true choice of change."[2]

Being at large does not consist in becoming another being among others but rather in projects of interpretation, in overcoming impositions that reduce our possibilities of freedom. Already at the beginning of the twentieth century, existentialist philosophers explained that the subject is not a metaphysical thing, a transcendental ego, or an idealist mind but rather a work in progress, a constant creation, and a project always beyond itself. For these reasons, our existence is at the centre of a set of meaningful relations comprehensible only against a larger background of social practices. These practices are historical, temporal, and contingent, making the subject fundamentally an interpretative being striving for freedom. If these features are vital for Being to be at large, that is, to resist impositions from above, it's because they are diametrically opposed to freedom understood as a property of man.

As Robert Nichols points out, a "movement is observable in the nineteenth and twentieth centuries ... not only toward questions of freedom, but also away from an understanding of freedom as a property of the subject and more as a practice or a relationship (something one does rather than has)."[3] This is why human freedom for Martin Heidegger "no longer means freedom as a property of man, but man as a possibility of freedom. Human freedom is the freedom that breaks through in man and takes him up unto itself, thus making man possible."[4] This condition does not entail the end of freedom but rather its beginning, insofar as this acknowledgment provides the starting point for an interpretative transformation of one's Being. Jean-Luc Nancy and Judith Butler, for example, acknowledge this when they separate freedom from any foundation and proprieties. The French philosopher designated freedom as "nothing more and nothing less than existence itself":

> Freedom, if it is something, is the very thing that prevents itself from being founded. The existence of God was to be free in the sense that the freedom that sustained his existence could not become one of its predicates or proprieties. Theology and philosophy had certainly recognized this limit, or this dilemma. Conceived of as freedom's necessary being, God risked (if one did not elaborate subtle *ad hoc* arguments) ruining both himself and freedom ... In return, a being taken for *being* as such, founding the freedom on which it is itself founded, designates the internal border of the limit of onto-theology: absolute subjectivity as the essence of essence, and of existence.[5]

An existence withdrawn from the logic of foundation implies a conception of freedom that is no only attuned to a deconstructed, unfounded, and dispersed Being but also anterior to any rational or juridical principle that might guarantee its practice. The fact that freedom is not something that can be appropriated indicates its embodiment in our performances and enactments:

When one freely exercises the right to be who one already is, and one asserts a social category for the purpose of describing that mode of being, then one is, in fact, making freedom part of that very social category, discursively changing the very ontology in question. When, long ago, I said that gender is performative, that meant that it is a certain kind of enactment, which means that one is not first one's gender and then later one decides how and when to enact it. The enactment is part of its very ontology, is a way of rethinking the ontological mode of gender, and so it matters how and when and with what consequences that enactment takes place, because all that changes the very gender that one "is."[6]

The performative nature of gender, as well as other existential enactments, is a consequence of being at large. When we are at large freedom becomes itself, that is, it comes to the fore independently of any foreign imposition. But in order for freedom to strive within our global framed order it must make an effort and take risks, that is, assume what remains of Being, interpretation's anarchic vein, and the absence of emergency as the greatest emergency. These features are not simply meant to "prevent freedom from being founded" but also to change "the very ontology in question."

History will continue to change the course of our lives, but it will also provide alternatives when necessary. But in order for this to happen we must promote emergencies. This does not mean becoming an armed terrorist and physically menacing the citizens of our framed global order; rather, we must strive to disclose those emergencies that are hidden by the "intellectual dark web" thinkers and their conservative agenda. This can take place through intellectual disruptions of our social, political, and cultural practices. When movements such as #MeToo, environmental groups such as Earth First!, and NGOs such as Proactiva Open Arms intervene within our global framed order we are thrust into emergencies that we are otherwise encouraged to ignore: social discrimination, ecological destruction, and the refugees crisis. What unites these positions is a different view not only of society but also of the effects our interpretations and participations can have.

The promotion and exposure of absent emergencies has become an existential affair that we must all endorse if we care about our freedom. The efforts and risks being at large implies are already part of the change that drives freedom in the first place. The sense of freedom expressed in Filippo Minelli's photographic artwork and the hacks in *Mr Robot* emerges because these interventions are at large, that is, unframed, unbound, and unpredictable. Being at large is the meaning of freedom in the age of alternative facts.

Notes

INTRODUCTION

1. Filippo Minelli's *Silent/Shapes* series is an ongoing project that began in 2009. See Freek Lomme, ed., *Passing to Presents: Silence and Golden in the Work of Filippo Minelli* (Eindhoven: Onomatopee, 2014). *Mr Robot* is a techno-thriller television series created by Sam Esmail and produced by the USA Network. The first three seasons ran from 24 June 2015 to 13 December 2017. A fourth and final season aired in 2019. Paul MacInnes, "Mr. Robot Creator Sam Esmail: 'The World Has Become Unreliable,'" *Guardian*, 17 October 2017, https://www.theguardian.com/tv-and-radio/2017/oct/17/mr-robot-creator-sam-esmail-the-world-has-become-unreliable.
2. Zygmunt Bauman, *Modernity and the Holocaust* (Ithaca: Cornell University Press, 1989), 93–4.
3. Richard Rorty, *Philosophy as Poetry* (Charlottesville: University of Virginia Press, 2016), 23.
4. Gianni Vattimo, *A Farewell to Truth*, trans. Robert Valgenti (New York: Columbia University Press, 2011), 77.
5. Bari Weiss, "Meet the Renegades of the Intellectual Dark Web," *New York Times*, 8 May 2018, https://www.nytimes.com/2018/05/08/opinion/intellectual-dark-web.html.
6. Christina Hoff Sommers, "How to Make Feminism Great Again," *Washington Post*, 5 December 2016. See also Christina Hoff Sommers, *Who Stole Feminism? How Women Have Betrayed Women* (New York: Simon & Schuster, 1994).

7 Jacob Hamburger, "The 'Intellectual Dark Web' Is Nothing New," *Los Angeles Review of Books*, 18 July 2018, https://lareviewofbooks.org/article/the-intellectual-dark-web-is-nothing-new/.
8 John Searle, *Freedom and Neurobiology* (New York: Columbia University Press, 2007), 32.
9 Graham Harman, *Guerrilla Metaphysics: Phenomenology and the Carpentry of Things* (Chicago: Open Court, 2005), 74.
10 Quentin Meillassoux, *After Finitude: An Essay on the Necessity of Contingency*, trans. Ray Brassier (London: Continuum, 2008), 7.
11 Simon Critchley, "Back to the Great Outdoors," *Times Literary Supplement*, 28 February 2009, 28.
12 Slavoj Žižek, *Disparities* (London: Bloomsbury, 2016), 102–3.
13 Gianni Vattimo, *Of Reality: The Purposes of Philosophy*, trans. Robert Valgenti (New York: Columbia University Press, 2016), 30.
14 Bruno Latour, *Down to Earth: Politics in the New Climate Regime*, trans. Catherine Porter (Cambridge: Polity, 2018), 23.
15 George Lakoff and Sean Illing, "How the Media Should Respond to Trump's Lies," *Vox*, 8 November 2018, https://www.vox.com/2018/11/15/18047360/trump-lies-media-strategy-george-lakoff.
16 Victor Davis Hanson, "Fake News: Postmodernism by Another Name," *Defining Ideas: A Hoover Institution Journal*, 26 January 2017, https://www.hoover.org/research/fake-news-postmodernism-another-name; Maurizio Ferraris, *Postverità e altri enigmi* (Bologna: Il Mulino, 2017).
17 Stanley Fish, "'Transparency' Is the Mother of Fake News," *New York Times*, 7 May 2018, https://www.nytimes.com/2018/05/07/opinion/transparency-fake-news.html.
18 Ibid.

PART ONE

1 As Peter Trawny explains, Heidegger's recently published *Black Notebooks* contain ideas that are "clearly antisemitic, even if it is not a question of antisemitism of the kind promoted by Nazi ideology." Trawny, "Eine neue Dimension," *Die Zeit*, 27 December 2013, 48. See also Trawny, *Heidegger and the Myth of a Jewish World Conspiracy*, trans. Andrew J. Mitchell (Chicago: University of Chicago Press,

2015); Domenico Losurdo, "Heidegger's 'Black Notebooks' Aren't That Surprising," *Guardian*, 19 March 2014, http://www.theguardian.com/commentisfree/2014/mar/19/heidegger-german-philosopher-black-books-not-surprising-nazi; Gregory Fried, "The King Is Dead: Heidegger's "Black Notebooks," *Los Angeles Review of Books*, 13 September 2014, https://lareviewofbooks.org/article/king-dead-heideggers-black-notebooks.

2. Jürgen Habermas and Michaël Foessel, "Critique and Communication: Philosophy's Missions: A conversation with Jürgen Habermas," trans. Alex J. Kay, *Eurozine*, 16 October 2015, https://www.eurozine.com/critique-and-communication-philosophys-missions/.

3. David Farrell Krell, *Ecstasy, Catastrophe: Heidegger from "Being and Time" to the "Black Notebooks"* (Albany, NY: SUNY Press, 2015), 158.

4. Fried, "The King Is Dead."

5. Martin Heidegger, "Martin Heidegger in Conversation," trans. Lisa Harries, in *Martin Heidegger and National Socialism: Questions and Answers*, eds. Günther Neske and Emil Kettering (New York: Paragon House, 1990), 82.

6. Jürgen Habermas, "Work and Weltanschauung: The Heidegger Controversy from a German Perspective," in *The New Conservatism: Cultural Criticism and the Historians' Debate*, ed. and trans. Shierry Weber Nicholsen (Cambridge, MA: MIT Press, 1989), 142–3.

7. Martin Heidegger, *Being and Time* (1927), trans. Joan Stambaugh (New York: SUNY Press 2010), 16.

8. Martin Heidegger, *Ponderings XII–XV: Black Notebooks 1939–1941*, trans. Richard Rojcewicz (Bloomington: Indiana University Press, 2017), 47–8.

9. Martin Heidegger, *Introduction to Metaphysics*, trans. Richard Polt and Gregory Fried (New Haven, CT: Yale University Press, 2000), 77.

10. Jean Grondin, *Introduction to Metaphysics: From Parmenides to Lévinas*, trans. Lukas Soderstrom (New York: Columbia University Press, 2012), xvii.

11. Heidegger, *Being and Time*, 22–3.

12. Martin Heidegger, *The Basic Problems of Phenomenology*, trans. Albert Hofstadter (Bloomington: Indiana University Press, 1982), 23.

13. Heidegger, *Being and Time*, 23.

14 Martin Heidegger, *On the Way to Language*, trans. Peter D. Hertz (New York: Harper & Row, 1982a), 32.
15 Martin Heidegger, *Basic Concepts*, trans. G.E. Aylesworth (Bloomington: Indiana University Press, 1993), 51–2.
16 Martin Heidegger, "Only a God Can Save Us," in *Martin Heidegger: Philosophical and Political Writings*, ed. Manfred Stassen (New York: Continuum, 2003), 37.
17 Martin Heidegger, *Pathmarks*, ed. William McNeill (Cambridge: Cambridge University Press, 2002), 251.
18 Heidegger, *Basic Concepts*, 51–2.
19 Heidegger, *Introduction to Metaphysics*, 77.
20 Polt and Fried in ibid., 56.
21 Charles Guignon, "Being as Appearing: Retrieving the Greek Experience of Phusis," in *A Companion to Heidegger's Introduction to Metaphysics*, eds. Richard Polt and Gregory Fried (New Haven, CT: Yale University Press, 2000), 34.
22 Heidegger, *Basic Concepts*, 52.
23 Heidegger, *Introduction to Metaphysics*, 219.
24 Hans-Georg Gadamer, "Reply to Jean Grondin," in *The Philosophy of Hans-Georg Gadamer*, ed. Lewis Edwin Hahn (Chicago: Open Court Press, 1997), 171.
25 Hans-Georg Gadamer, *The Gadamer Reader: A Bouquet of the Later Writings*, ed. Jean Grondin, trans. Richard Palmer (Evanston, IL: Northwestern University Press, 2007), 382.
26 Hans-Georg Gadamer, *Dialogue and Deconstruction: The Gadamer-Derrida Encounter*, eds. Diane P. Michelfelder and Richard Palmer (Albany, NY: SUNY Press, 1989), 100.
27 Martin Heidegger, *On Time and Being*, trans. Joan Stambaugh (Chicago: University of Chicago Press, 2002), 91.
28 Martin Heidegger, *Ontology: The Hermeneutics of Facticity*, trans. John van Buren (Bloomington: Indiana University Press, 1999), 14–16.
29 Heidegger, *Introduction to Metaphysics*, 90.
30 Ibid., 86.
31 Jacques Derrida, *Margins of Philosophy*, trans. Alan Bass (Chicago: University of Chicago Press, 1982), 177.
32 Jacques Derrida, *Of Grammatology*, trans. Gayatri Chakravorty Spivak (Baltimore, MD: John Hopkins University Press, 1997), 22.

33 Jacques Derrida, *Margins of Philosophy*, trans. Alan Bass (Chicago: University of Chicago Press, 1982), 3.
34 Ibid., 22.
35 Ibid., 5.
36 Derrida, *Of Grammatology*, 62–3.
37 Derrida, *Positions*, trans. Alan Bass (London: Continuum, 2002), 26.
38 Derrida, *Points … Interviews 1974–1994*, ed. Elisabeth Weber, trans. Peggy Kamuf and others (Stanford, CA: Stanford University Press, 1995), 208.
39 Jacques Derrida, *Margins of Philosophy*, trans. Alan Bass (Chicago: University of Chicago Press, 1982), 5–6.
40 Gianni Vattimo, *The End of Modernity: Nihilism and Hermeneutics in Postmodern Culture*, trans. John Snyder (Baltimore: John Hopkins University Press, 1988), 86.
41 Gianni Vattimo and Santiago Zabala, "Weak Thought and the Reduction of Violence: A Dialogue with Gianni Vattimo," trans. Yaakov Mascetti, *Common Knowledge* no.3 (2002): 463.
42 Gianni Vattimo, foreword to Franca D'Agostini, *Analitici e continentali. Guida alla filosofia degli ultimi trent'anni* (Milan: Cortina, 1997), x.
43 Gianni Vattimo, *The Adventure of Difference: Philosophy After Nietzsche and Heidegger*, trans. Cyprian Blamires and Thomas Harrison (Cambridge: Polity Press, 1993), 5.
44 Gianni Vattimo, "Dialectics, Difference, and Weak Thought," trans. Thomas Harrison, *Graduate Faculty Philosophy Journal* no. 10 (1984): 151.
45 Gianni Vattimo, "Difference and Interference: on the Reduction of Hermeneutics to Anthropology," *Res no.* 4 (1982): 88.
46 Gianni Vattimo, *Art's Claim to Truth*, ed. Santiago Zabala, trans. Luca D'Isanto (New York: Columbia University Press, 2008), 148.
47 Gianni Vattimo, *Beyond Interpretation: The Meaning of Hermeneutics for Philosophy*, trans. David Webb (Cambridge: Polity Press, 1997), 105.
48 For an account of this new question, see Santiago Zabala, *The Remains of Being: Hermeneutic Ontology after Metaphysics* (New York: Columbia University Press, 2009).
49 Martin Heidegger, *The Concept of Time*, trans. William McNeill (London: Wiley-Blackwell, 1992), 20.

50 Michael Bowler and Ingo Farin, eds., *Hermeneutical Heidegger* (Evanston, IL: Northwestern University Press, 2016), 4.
51 Richard Rorty, "Being That Can Be Understood Is Language," in *Gadamer's Repercussion: Reconsidering Philosophical Hermeneutics*, ed. Bruce Krajewski (Berkeley: University of California Press, 2004), 29.
52 Hans-Georg Gadamer, "Subjectivity and Intersubjectivity, Subject and Person," trans. Peter Adamson and David Vessey, *Continental Philosophy Review* no. 33 (2000): 277–88.
53 Gadamer, *The Gadamer Reader*, 371.
54 Richard Rorty and Gianni Vattimo, *The Future of Religion*, ed. Santiago Zabala (New York: Columbia University Press, 2005), 68.
55 Gianni Vattimo, *After Christianity*, trans. Luca D'Isanto (New York: Columbia University Press, 2002), 67.
56 Heidegger, *Introduction to Metaphysics*, 90.
57 Heidegger, *Being and Time*, xvii.
58 Ibid., 10.
59 Otto Pöggeler, "Heideggers logische Untersuchungen," in *Martin Heidegger: Innen-und Aussenansichten. Forum für Philosophie Bad Hamburg* (Frankfurt: M. Suhrkamp, 1989), 75–100; my translation.
60 Hans-Georg Gadamer, *The Beginning of Philosophy*, trans. Rod Coltman (New York: Continuum, 2001), 123.
61 Martin Heidegger, *Off the Beaten Track*, eds. and trans. Julian Young and Kenneth Haynes (Cambridge: Cambridge University Press, 2002), 275.
62 Martin Heidegger, *What Is Philosophy?*, trans. Jean T. Wilde and William Kluback (New York: Rowman & Littlefield, 2003), 71–3.
63 Heidegger, *On Time and Being*, 3.
64 Martin Heidegger, *The Question Concerning Technology*, trans. William Lovitt (New York: Harper & Row, 1977), 39.
65 Heidegger, *Basic Concepts*, 52.
66 Heidegger, *On Time and Being*, 24.
67 Heidegger, *Ontology: The Hermeneutics of Facticity*, 16.
68 Heidegger, *On the Way to Language*, 32.
69 Richard Rorty, *Essays on Heidegger and Others* (Cambridge: Cambridge University Press, 1991), 6.
70 Richard Rorty, *Philosophy as Cultural Politics* (Cambridge: Cambridge University Press, 2007), 129.

71 Vattimo, *After Christianity*, 67–78.
72 Vattimo, *Beyond Interpretation*, 7.
73 Richard Rorty, *Philosophy and the Mirror of Nature* (Princeton, NJ: Princeton University Press, 1979; 2009), 315.
74 Ibid., 325.
75 Georgia Warnke, "Hermeneutics and the Social Sciences: A Gadamerian Critique of Rorty," in *Inquiry* 28 (September, 1985), 341.
76 Jean Grondin, "Vattimo's Latinization of Hermeneutics: Why Did Gadamer Resist Postmodernism?" in *Weakening Philosophy*, ed. Santiago Zabala (Montreal: McGill-Queen's University Press, 2007), 211.
77 Martin Heidegger, letter to Otto Pöggeler, 5 January 1973, in Pöggeler, *Heidegger und die Hermeneutische Philosophie* (Freiburg: Alber, 1973), 395.
78 Rorty, "Being That Can Be Understood Is Language," 21.
79 Hans-Georg Gadamer, "Reflections on My Philosophical Journey," in *The Philosophy of Hans-Georg Gadamer*, ed. Lewis Edwin Hahn (Chicago: Open Court Press, 1997), 22.
80 James Risser, "Dialogue and Conversation," in *Routledge Companion to Hermeneutics*, eds. Jeff Malpas and Hans-Helmut Gander (London: Routledge, 2015), 341.
81 Gadamer, "Reflections on My Philosophical Journey," 30.
82 Gadamer, "Reply to Jean Grondin," 171–2.
83 Gadamer, *Dialogue and Deconstruction*, 118–22.
84 Rorty, *Philosophy and the Mirror of Nature*, 389.
85 Vattimo, *A Farewell to Truth*, xxxi, xxxii.
86 Jean Grondin, *Introduction to Philosophical Hermeneutics*, trans. Joel Weinsheimer (New Haven, CT: Yale University Press, 1994), 91.
87 Theodore Kisiel, *The Genesis of Heidegger's Being and Time* (Berkeley: University of California Press, 1993), 21.
88 Martin Heidegger, *Logic: The Question of Truth*, trans. Thomas Sheehan (Bloomington: University of Indiana Press, 2010), 137.
89 Ernst Tugendhat, *Ti Kata Tinos: Eine Untersuchung zu Struktur und Ursprung Aristotelischer Grundbegriffe* (Freiburg: Verlag Karl Alber, 1958); my translation.
90 Ernst Tugendhat, *Self-Consciousness and Self-Determination*, trans. Paul Stern (Cambridge, MA: MIT Press, 1986), 284–5.

91 Ernst Tugendhat, *Der Wahrheitsbegriff bei Husserl und Heidegger* (Berlin: Walter de Gruyter, 1967, 1970, 1983), 1; my translation.
92 Heidegger, *Being and Time*, 207–8.
93 Santiago Zabala, *The Hermeneutic Nature of Analytical Philosophy: A Study of Ernst Tugendhat* (New York: Columbia University Press, 2008), 29.
94 Ernst Tugendhat, *Der Wahrheitsbegriff bei Husserl und Heidegger* (Berlin: Walter de Gruyter, 2011), 350.
95 Karl-Otto Apel, "Regulative Ideas or Truth-Happening? An Attempt to Answer the Question of the Conditions of the Possibility of Valid Understanding," in *The Philosophy of Hans-Georg Gadamer*, ed. Lewis Edwin Hahn (Chicago: Open Court, 1997), 67–94.
96 Heidegger, *On Time and Being*, 70.
97 Barry Allen, *Truth in Philosophy* (Cambridge, MA: Harvard University Press, 1993), 89.
98 John Sallis, "The Truth Is Not of Knowledge," in *Reading Heidegger from the Start*, eds. Theodore Kisiel and John van Buren (Albany, NY: SUNY Press, 1994), 390.
99 Heidegger, *Being and Time*, 208.
100 Gianni Vattimo, *The Responsibility of the Philosopher*, trans. Luca D'Isanto (New York: Columbia University Press, 2010), 60.
101 Heidegger, *Pathmarks*, 145.
102 Martin Heidegger, *The Essence of Human Freedom*, trans. Ted Sadler (London: Continuum, 2002), 94.
103 Martin Heidegger, *Mindfulness*, trans. Parvis Emad and Thomas Kalary (New York: Continuum, 2006), 31.
104 Brice Wachterhauser, "Introduction: Is There Truth after Interpretation?" in *Hermeneutics and Truth*, ed. Brice Wachterhauser (Evanston, IL: Northwestern University Press, 1994), 4.
105 Heidegger, *Mindfulness*, 31.
106 Jacques Derrida, *Paper Machine*, trans. Rachel Bowlby (Stanford, CA: Stanford University Press, 2005), 151–2.
107 Jean-Luc Nancy, *The Sense of the World*, trans. Jeffrey S. Librett (Minneapolis: University of Minnesota Press, 1997), 132.
108 Reiner Schürmann, *Heidegger on Being and Acting: From Principles to Anarchy*, trans. Christine-Marie Gros (Bloomington: University of Indiana Press, 1990), 49.

PART TWO

1 According to J. Grondin, a renowned disciple of Gadamer, Nietzsche should not be included within the hermeneutic tradition; see "Must Nietzsche Be Incorporated into Hermeneutics? Some Reasons for a Little Resistance," *Iris: European Journal of Philosophy and Public Debate* 2, no. 3 (April 2010): 105–22. While Grondin, together with Richard Palmer and Kurt Mueller-Vollmer do not believe Nietzsche should be included within the hermeneutic tradition, a number of other scholars have given the German thinker a central place within the discipline; see Maurizio Ferraris, *History of Hermeneutics*, trans. L. Somigli (Englewood Cliffs, NJ: Humanities Press, 1996); Gayle L. Ormiston and Alan D. Schrift, eds. *The Hermeneutic Tradition: from Ast to Ricoeur* (Albany, NY: SUNY Press, 1990); Gayle L. Ormiston and Alan D. Schrift, *Transforming the Hermeneutic Context: From Nietzsche to Nancy* (Albany, NY: SUNY Press 1990); Alan Douglas Schrift, *Nietzsche and the Question of Interpretation: Between Hermeneutics and Deconstruction* (New York: Routledge, 1990).
2 Gianni Vattimo, *Essere e dintorni*, eds. Alberto Martinengo, Giuseppe Iannantuono, and Santiago Zabala (Milan: La Nave di Teseo, 2018), 88, originally published in English as "The Political Outcome of Hermeneutics," in *Consequences of Hermeneutics*, eds. Jeff Malpas and Santiago Zabala (Evanston, IL: Northwestern University Press, 2010), 282.
3 See Sara Heinämaa, "Hermeneutics and Feminist Philosophy," in *The Blackwell Companion to Hermeneutics*, eds. Niall Keane and Chris Lawn (London: Wiley-Blackwell, 2017), 557–67; Gianni Vattimo and Santiago Zabala, *Hermeneutic Communism: From Heidegger to Marx* (New York: Columbia University Press, 2011); Forrest Clingerman, Brian Treanor, Martin Drenthen, and David Utsler, eds., *Interpreting Nature: The Emerging Field of Environmental Hermeneutics* (New York: Fordham University Press, 2013); John D. Caputo, *Hermeneutics: Facts and Interpretation in the Age of Information* (London: Pelican, 2018).
4 Hans-Georg Gadamer, *Truth and Method*, trans. Joel Weinsheimer and Donald G. Marshall (London: Continuum, 2014), 286–91.

5 Jeff Malpas, "Introduction: Hermeneutics and Philosophy," in *The Routledge Companion to Hermeneutics*, eds. Jeff Malpas and Hans-Helmuth Gander (London: Routledge, 2015), 3.
6 Martin Heidegger, *Ontology: The Hermeneutics of Facticity*, trans. John van Buren (Bloomington: Indiana University Press, 1999), 9.
7 Kathy Eden, *Hermeneutics and the Rhetorical Tradition: Chapters in the Ancient Legacy and Its Humanist Reception* (New Haven, CT: Yale University Press, 1997), 2.
8 Malpas, "Introduction: Hermeneutics and Philosophy," 5.
9 Vattimo, *Essere e dintorni*, 72, originally published in English as "The Future of Hermeneutics" in *The Routledge Companion to Hermeneutics*, eds. Jeff Malpas and Hans-Helmuth Gander (London: Routledge, 2015), 722.
10 Gerald L. Bruns, *Hermeneutics: Ancient and Modern* (New Haven, CT: Yale University Press, 1992), 17.
11 Ibid., 215.
12 Francisco Gonzalez, "Hermeneutics in Greek Philosophy," in *The Routledge Companion to Hermeneutics*, eds. Jeff Malpas and Hans-Helmuth Gander (London: Routledge, 2015), 13.
13 Jean Greisch, "Hermeneutics, Religion, and God," in *The Routledge Companion to Hermeneutics*, eds. Jeff Malpas and Hans-Helmuth Gander (London: Routledge, 2015), 439. On Hermes, see Maurizio Bettini, *The Ears of Hermes. Communication, Images, and Identity in the Classical World*, trans. Michael Short (Columbus: Ohio State University Press, 2011).
14 Wilhelm Dilthey, *Hermeneutics and the Study of History*, eds. Rudolf A. Makkreel and Frithjof Rodi, vol. IV: Selected Works (Princeton, NJ: Princeton University Press, 1996); Friedrich Schleiermacher, *Hermeneutics and Criticism and Other Writings*, ed. and trans. Andrew Bowie (Cambridge: Cambridge University Press, 1998), 14.
15 Friedrich Nietzsche, *The Will to Power*, trans. W. Kaufmann and R. J. Hollingdale (London: Weidenfeld and Nicolson, 1968), 267.
16 Hans-Georg Gadamer, *The Gadamer Reader: A Bouquet of the Later Writings*, ed. Richard Palmer (Evanston, IL: Northwestern University Press, 2007), 181.

17 Vattimo, *Essere e dintorni*, 79, originally published in English as "The Future of Hermeneutics," 725.
18 For Schürmann, "anarchy means absence of rule, but not absence of rules"; Reiner Schürmann, *Heidegger on Being and Acting: From Principles to Anarchy* (Bloomington: Indiana University Press, 1990, 295).
19 Simon Critchley, introduction to *The Anarchist Turn*, eds. Jacob Blumenfeld, Chiara Bottici, and Simon Critchley (New York: Pluto, 2013), 4.
20 John D. Caputo, *Hermeneutics: Facts and Interpretation in the Age of Information* (London: Pelican Books, 2018), 173.
21 A detailed account of Vattimo's philosophy and life is available in Gianni Vattimo, *Not Being God: A Collaborative Autobiography*, with Piergiorgio Paterlini, trans. William McCuaig (New York: Columbia University Press, 2009); and Santiago Zabala, ed., *Weakening Philosophy* with contributions from Umberto Eco, Jean-Luc Nancy, and others (Montreal: McGill-Queen's University Press, 2007). Neil Gross, *Richard Rorty: The Making of an American Philosopher* (Chicago: University of Chicago Press, 2008), provides a detailed account of his role within the philosophical community. See also Santiago Zabala, ed., "Conversational Philosophy: A Forum on Richard Rorty," with contributions from Martin Woessner, Marianne Janack, Maria Pía Lara, Eduardo Mendieta, and Martin Woessner, *Los Angeles Review of Books*, 22 July 2017, https://lareviewofbooks.org/feature/conversational-philosophy-forum-richard-rorty/.
22 Robert Valgenti, "Vattimo at 80: A Hermeneutic Reality Check," *Philosophy Today* 60, no. 3 (Summer 2016): 618.
23 Vattimo, *Essere e dintorni*, 75, originally published in English as "The Future of Hermeneutics," 723–4.
24 Vattimo, *Essere e dintorni*, 30–1, originally published in English as "Insuperable Contradictions and Events," in *Being Shaken*, eds. Michael Marder and Santiago Zabala (London: Palgrave Macmillan, 2014) 73.
25 James Risser, "On the Continuation of Philosophy: Hermeneutics as Convalescence," in *Weakening Philosophy: Essays in Honor of Gianni*

Vattimo, ed. Santiago Zabala (Montreal: McGill-Queen's University Press, 2007), 184–5.

26 Vattimo, *Essere e dintorni*, 83, originally published in English as "The Future of Hermeneutics," 727.

27 Gianni Vattimo, "The Age of Interpretation," in Richard Rorty and Gianni Vattimo, *The Future of Religion*, ed. Santiago Zabala (New York: Columbia University Press, 2006), 130.

28 Gianni Vattimo, *Dialogue with Nietzsche*, trans. William McCuaig (New York: Columbia University Press. 2006), 130.

29 Gianni Vattimo, *Essere e dintorni*, 325, originally published in English as "Gadamer and the Problem of Ontology," in *Gadamer's Century*, eds. Jeff Malpas, Ulrich Arnswald, and Jens Kertscher (Cambridge, MA: MIT Press, 2002), 299.

30 Gianni Vattimo, *Of Reality*, trans. Robert Valgenti (New York: Columbia University Press, 2016), 184.

31 Vattimo, *Essere e dintorni*, 95, originally published in English as "The Political Outcome of Hermeneutics: To Politics through Art and Religion," in *Consequences of Hermeneutics: Fifty Years after Gadamer's "Truth and Method"*, eds. Jeff Malpas and Santiago Zabala (Evanston, IL: Northwestern University Press, 2010), 286.

32 Vattimo, *Essere e dintorni*, 73–4, originally published in English as "The Future of Hermeneutics," 723–4.

33 David Webb, "Vattimo's Hermeneutics as a Practice of Freedom," in *Between Nihilism and Politics: The Hermeneutics of Gianni Vattimo*, eds. Silvia Benso and Brian Schroeder (Albany, NY: SUNY Press, 2010), 57.

34 Gianni Vattimo, *Essere e dintorni*, 83, published in English as "The Future of Hermeneutics," 727.

35 Martin Woessner, "Rorty and Social and Hope," *Los Angeles Review of Books*, 22 July 2017, https://lareviewofbooks.org/article/rorty-social-hope.

36 Rorty, *Philosophy as Poetry*, 42–3.

37 Richard Rorty, *Philosophy and the Mirror of Nature* (Princeton, NJ: Princeton University Press, 1979; 2009), 318.

38 Richard Rorty, "Hermeneutics, General Studies, and Teaching," in C. Barry Chabot, *Richard Rorty on General Studies and Teaching* (Fairfax, VA: George Mason University, 1982), 14.

39 Jane Heal, "Pragmatism and Choosing to Believe," in *Reading Rorty: Critical Responses to Philosophy and the Mirror of Nature (and Beyond)*, ed. Alan A. Malachowski (Oxford: Blackwell, 1990), 103.
40 Rorty, *Philosophy and the Mirror of Nature*, 359.
41 Ibid., 322–3.
42 Ibid., 364–5.
43 Richard Rorty, ed., *The Linguistic Turn* (Chicago: Chicago University Press, 1967), 1.
44 Richard Rorty, 1976 National Endowment for the Humanities seminar notes, Papers of Richard Rorty, Stanford University (Stanford, Calif.)
45 On this matter see John McCumber, *Time in the Ditch: American Philosophy and the McCarthy Era* (Evanston, IL: Northwestern University Press, 2001).
46 Richard Rorty to Members of the Eastern Division APA Executive Committee, 15 June 1979, Papers of Richard Rorty, Stanford University (Stanford, Calif.).
47 Neil Gross, *Richard Rorty: The Making of an American Philosopher* (Chicago: University of Chicago Press, 2008), 217.
48 Richard Rorty, *Consequences of Pragmatism* (Minneapolis: University of Minnesota Press, 2019), 219.
49 It must be pointed out that Michel Foucault grouped together Marx, Nietzsche, and Freud as "masters of suspicion" before Ricoeur in his 1964 article "Nietzsche, Freud, Marx," reprinted in Gayle L. Ormiston and Alan D. Schrift, eds., *Transforming the Hermeneutic Context* (Albany, NY: SUNY Press, 1990), 59–67. On the relation between Freud and Nietzsche see Ronald Lehrer, *Nietzsche's Presence in Freud's Life and Thought* (Albany, NY: SUNY Press, 1995); Élisabeth Roudinesco, *Freud in His Time and Ours*, trans. C. Porter (Cambridge, MA: Harvard University Press, 2016); and Rüdiger Safranski, *Nietzsche: A Philosophical Biography*, trans. S. Frisch (New York: Norton, 2003).
50 Roudinesco, *Freud in His Time and Ours*, 81.
51 Sigmund Freud, *The Standard Edition of the Complete Psychological Works of Sigmund Freud*, vol. 18, *1920–1922: Beyond the Pleasure Principle, Group Psychology, and Other Works*, eds. and trans. James Strachey and Anna Freud (London: The Hogarth Press, 1955), 235.
52 Sigmund Freud, "Project for a Scientific Psychology," in *The Standard Edition of the Complete Psychological Works of Sigmund Freud*,

vol. 1, *1886–1899: Pre-Psycho-Analytic Publications and Unpublished Drafts*, eds. and trans. James Strachey and Anna Freud (London: The Hogarth Press, 1955), 295.

53 Sigmund Freud, *The Standard Edition of the Complete Psychological Works of Sigmund Freud*, vol. 17, *1917–1919: An Infantile Neurosis and Other Works*, eds. and trans. James Strachey and Anna Freud (London: The Hogarth Press, 1955), 160.

54 Anthony Storr, *Freud: A Very Short Introduction* (Oxford: Oxford University Press, 1989), 16.

55 Eli Zaretsky, *Political Freud: A History* (New York: Columbia University Press, 2015), 186.

56 Élisabeth Roudinesco reports that Freud became acquainted very early with the sacred text as his parents (Jacob and Amalia) initiated him into the "biblical narrative as if it were a genealogical family novel, which gave the young Freud intense pleasure. Throughout his school days he continued to immerse himself in the biblical language, especially through his contact with Samuel Hammerschlag, his Hebrew professor, who also helped him finance his studies." Élisabeth Roudinesco, *Freud in His Time and Ours*, trans. C. Porter (Cambridge: Harvard University Press, 2016), 14.

57 Philippe Cabestan, "Hermeneutics and Psychoanalysis," in *The Routledge Companion to Hermeneutics*, eds. Jeff Malpas and Hans-Helmuth Gander (London: Routledge, 2015), 624.

58 Sigmund Freud, *The Standard Edition of the Complete Psychological Works of Sigmund Freud*, vol. 4, *1900–1901: The Interpretation of Dreams*, eds. and trans. James Strachey and Anna Freud (London: The Hogarth Press, 1955), 277.

59 Freud, *An Infantile Neurosis and Other Works*, 160.

60 Roudinesco, *Freud in His Time and Ours*, 352–3.

61 Thomas Mann, *Freud's Position in the History of Modern Thought* (London: Burns Oates and Washbourne, 1929; 1933). See also Lehrer, *Nietzsche's Presence in Freud's Life and Thought*; and Jacob Golomb, Weaver Santaniello, and Ronald Lehrer, eds., *Nietzsche and Depth Psychology* (Albany, NY: SUNY Press, 1999).

62 Quoted in Ernest Jones, *The Life and Work of Sigmund Freud*, vol. 2, *1901–1919: Years of Maturity* (New York: Basic Books, 1955), 385.

63 Sigmund Freud, *The Standard Edition of the Complete Psychological Works of Sigmund Freud*, vol. 20, 1925–1926: *An Autobiographical Study, Inhibitions, Symptoms and Anxiety, The Question of Lay Analysis and Other Works*, eds. and trans. James Strachey and Anna Freud, 59–60.
64 Friedrich Nietzsche, *On the Genealogy of Morals*, in *Basic Writings of Nietzsche*, ed. and trans. Walter Kaufmann (New York: Modern Library, 2000), 451.
65 Jacob Golomb, "Introductory Essay: Nietzsche's 'New Psychology,'" in *Nietzsche and Depth Psychology*, eds. Jacob Golomb, Weaver Santaniello, and Ronald Lehrer (Albany, NY: SUNY Press, 1999), 5.
66 Ibid., 4.
67 See Walter A. Kaufmann, *Nietzsche: Philosopher, Psychologist, Antichrist* (Princeton: Princeton University Press, 2013); and Robert B. Pippin, *Nietzsche, Psychology, and First Philosophy* (Chicago and London: University Press of Chicago, 2010).
68 Eric Blondel, "Nietzsche and Freud, or: How to Be within Philosophy While Criticizing It from Without," in *Nietzsche and Depth Psychology*, eds. Jacob Golomb, Weaver Santaniello, and Ronald Lehrer (Albany, NY: SUNY Press, 1999), 174.
69 Friedrich Nietzsche, "Homer and Classical Philology," in *The Complete Works of Friedrich Nietzsche*, Volume III, ed. Oscar Levy (New York: Macmillan, 1910). This sentence was translated by Babette Babich.
70 Friedrich Nietzsche, *Sämtliche Werke. Kritische Gesamtausgabe*, eds. Giorgio Colli and Mazzino Montinari (Berlin: de Gruyter, 1967), 1.4 52 (30), spring 1867–winter 1868.
71 Babette Babich, "Nietzsche," in *The Blackwell Companion to Hermeneutics*, eds. Niall Keane and Chris Lawn (London: Wiley-Blackwell, 2016), 367.
72 Friedrich Nietzsche, "On the Uses and Disadvantages of History for Life," in *Untimely Meditations*, ed. Daniel Breazeale, trans. Reginald J. Hollingdale (Cambridge: Cambridge University Press, 1983), 67.
73 Vattimo, *Dialogue with Nietzsche*, 79.
74 Nietzsche, *The Will to Power*, 267.

75 Alan Schrift, *Nietzsche and the Question of Interpretation* (New York: Routledge, 1990), 145.
76 Friedrich Nietzsche, *On Truth and Untruth: Selected Writings*, ed. and trans. Taylor Carman (New York: Harper Perennial Modern Thought, 2010), 36–7.
77 Jean Granier, "Perspectivism and Interpretation," in *The New Nietzsche*, ed. David B. Allison (New York: Delta, 1977), 191–200.
78 Jean Grondin, *Introduction to Philosophical Hermeneutics*, trans. Joel Weinsheimer (New Haven, CT: Yale University Press, 1994), 32–3.
79 Hans-Georg Gadamer, *Truth and Method* (1960), trans. Joel Weinsheimer and Donald G. Marshall (London: Continuum, 2004), 279.
80 Lyndal Roper, *Martin Luther: Renegade and Prophet* (New York: Random House, 2018), xix.
81 Martin Luther, *Luther's Works: Word and Sacrament* II, vol. 36, eds. H. Lehmann and A. Wentz (Philadelphia: Fortress Press, 1959), 107.
82 Michael Massing, *Fatal Discord: Erasmus, Luther, and the Fight for the Western Mind* (New York: Harper, 2018), x.
83 Jens Zimmermann, "Martin Luther," in *The Blackwell Companion to Hermeneutics*, eds. Niall Keane and Chris Lawn (London: Wiley-Blackwell, 2016), 335.
84 Martin Luther, "Assertio Omnium Articulorum Martini Lutheri Per Bullam Leonis X: Novissiman Damnatorum (1520)," in *Lateinisch-Deutsche Studienausgabe: Der Mensch vor Gott*, vol. 1, eds. Wilfried Härle, Johannes Schilling, and Günther Wartenberg (Leipzig: Evangelische Verlagsanstalt, 2006), 77.
85 Martin Luther, "Heidelberger Disputation, XX," in *Lateinisch-Deutsche Studienausgabe: Der Mensch vor Gott*, 53.
86 Martin Luther, "Vorrede auf das Alte Testament," in *Luthers Vorreden zur Bibel*, ed. Heinrich Bornkamm (Göttingen: Vandenhoeck & Ruprecht, 1989), 56.
87 Grondin, *Introduction to Philosophical Hermeneutics*, 40.
88 David Jasper, *A Short Introduction to Hermeneutics* (Louisville, KY: Westminster John Knox Press, 2004), 56.

89 Massing, *Fatal Discord*, 252.
90 Dennis J. Schmidt, "Text and Translation," in *The Routledge Companion to Hermeneutics*, eds. Jeff Malpas and Hans-Helmuth Gander (London: Routledge, 2015) 350.
91 Massing, *Fatal Discord*, 527.
92 Ibid., 554.
93 Heidegger, *Ontology: The Hermeneutics of Facticity*, 10.
94 Gerhard Ebeling, "Art: Hermeneutik," in *Die Religion in Geschichte und Gegenwart*, 3rd ed. (Tubingen: Mohr, 1959), 249.
95 Augustine, *On Christian Doctrine*, book 3, trans. D.W. Robertson (Indianapolis: Bobbs-Merrill, 1958), 78.
96 Augustine, *On Christian Doctrine*, book 1, trans. D.W. Robertson (Indianapolis: Bobbs-Merrill, 1958), 40–1.
97 Thomas Williams, "Biblical Interpretation," in *Cambridge Companion to Augustine*, eds. Elenore Stump and Norman Kretzmann (Cambridge: Cambridge University Press, 2001), 59.
98 Jean Grondin, *Introduction to Philosophical Hermeneutics*, trans. Joel Weinsheimer (New Haven, CT: Yale University Press, 1994), 34. See also Jean Grondin, "Gadamer and Augustine," in *Sources of Hermeneutics* (Albany, NY: SUNY Press, 1995), 99–110.
99 Augustine, *On Christian Doctrine*, book 3, 9.
100 Bruns, *Hermeneutics: Ancient and Modern*, 143.
101 Augustine, *On Christian Doctrine*, book 1, 9.
102 David Jasper, *A Short Introduction to Hermeneutics* (Louisville, KY: Westminster John Knox Press, 2004), 41.
103 Gadamer, *Truth and Method*, 438.
104 Grondin, *Introduction to Philosophical Hermeneutics*, 37.
105 Augustine, *On the Free Choice of the Will, On Grace and Free Choice, and Other Writings*, ed. and trans. Peter King (Cambridge: Cambridge University Press, 2010), 5.
106 Augustine, *On Christian Doctrine*, book 1, 37, 41.
107 Kathy Eden, *Hermeneutics and the Rhetorical Tradition: Chapters in the Ancient Legacy and Its Humanist Reception* (New Haven, CT: Yale University Press, 1997), 54.
108 Williams, "Biblical Interpretation," 69.

PART THREE

1 Tracy B. Strong, foreword to Carl Schmitt, *Political Theology*, trans. George Schwab (Chicago: University of Chicago Press, 1985), xiii, xiv.
2 Ibid., 5.
3 Walter Benjamin, "Theses on the Philosophy of History," in *Illuminations*, trans. Harry Zohn (New York: Schocken, 1969), 248.
4 Giorgio Agamben, *Stato di eccezione* (Turin: Bollati Boringhieri, 2003). English translation: *State of Exception*, trans. Kevin Attell (Chicago: University of Chicago Press, 2005).
5 Martin Heidegger, *Contributions to Philosophy (Of the Event)* (1989), trans. Parvis Emad and Kenneth Maly (Bloomington: Indiana University Press, 1989; 1999), 87.
6 Martin Heidegger, *Contributions to Philosophy (Of the Event)*, trans. Richard Rojcewicz and Daniela Vallega-Neu (Bloomington: Indiana University Press, 2012), 99.
7 This quote is from Richard Polt, *The Emergency of Being* (Ithaca, NY: Cornell University Press, 2006), 219, where, as we can see, he opted for "emergency" rather than "distress" or "plight."
8 Giorgio Agamben, *State of Exception*, 52. While Agamben sees Schmitt's *Political Theology* as an attempt to capture Benjamin's pure anomic violence and reinscribe that violence within a juridical context, others (such as Ellen Kennedy in *Constitutional Failure: Carl Schmitt in Weimar* [Durham, NC: Duke University Press, 2004]) believe he was more likely concerned with the liberalism and legal positivism of Hans Kelsen's *The Problem of Sovereignty and the Theory of International Law* (1920).
9 Colin McQuillan, "The Real State of Emergency: Agamben on Benjamin and Schmitt," *Studies in Social and Political Thought* 18 (Winter 2011): 99.
10 Ibid.
11 Walter Benjamin, *Illuminations*, trans. Harry Zohn (New York: Schocken, 1969), 248–9; and Walter Benjamin, *On the Concept of History*, in Walter Benjamin, *Selected Writings*, vol. 4, 1938–1940, trans. H. Zohn (Cambridge: Harvard University Press. 2003), 407, 396, 395.

12 Benjamin, *Illuminations*, 248.
13 Ibid., 249.
14 Ibid., 248.
15 Michael Löwy, *Fire Alarm: Reading Walter Benjamin's "On the Concept of History"*, trans. Chris Turner (London: Verso, 2005), 58.
16 Walter Benjamin, *The Origin of the German Tragic Drama*, trans. J. Osborne (New York: Verso, 2003), 71.
17 Walter Benjamin, *The Origin of the German Tragic Drama*, trans. Kevin Attell (Chicago: University of Chicago Press, 2005), 54.
18 Saul Newman, *Political Theology: A Critical Introduction* (London: Polity, 2019), 54.
19 Carl Schmitt, *Roman Catholicism and Political Form*, trans. Gary L. Ulmen (Westport, CT: Greenwood Press, 1996), 20.
20 Carl Schmitt, *The Crisis of Parliamentary Democracy*, trans. Ellen Kennedy (Cambridge, MA: MIT Press, 2000), 35.
21 Carl Schmitt, *Political Theology: Four Chapters on the Concept of Sovereignty*, trans. and ed. George Schwab (Chicago: University of Chicago Press, 2006), 15.
22 Newman, *Political Theology: A Critical Introduction*, 29.
23 Schmitt, *Political Theology: Four Chapters on the Concept of Sovereignty*, 6–7.
24 Giorgio Agamben, "De l'Etat de droit à l'Etat de sécurité," *Le Monde*, 23 December 2015, https://www.lemonde.fr/idees/article/2015/12/23/de-l-etat-de-droit-a-l-etat-de-securite_4836816_3232.html; my translation.
25 Agamben, *State of Exception*, 54.
26 Ibid., 11.
27 Adam Kotsko, "How to Read Agamben," *Los Angeles Review of Books*, 4 June 2013, https://lareviewofbooks.org/article/how-to-read-agamben/.
28 Giorgio Agamben, *Homo Sacer: Sovereign Power and Bare Life*, trans. Daniel Heller-Roazen (Stanford, CA: Stanford University Press, 1998), 19.
29 David Kishik, *The Power of Life: Agamben and the Coming Politics*, vol. 2, *To Imagine a Form of Life* (Stanford, CA: Stanford University Press, 2012), 19.
30 Agamben, *Homo Sacer: Sovereign Power and Bare Life*, 84.

31 Giorgio Agamben, *Means Without End: Notes on Politics*, trans. Vincenzo Binetti and Casate Casarino (Minneapolis: University of Minnesota Press, 2000), 40.
32 Agamben, *State of Exception*, 86.
33 Bruno Gullì, "The Ontology and Politics of Exception: Reflections on the Work of Giorgio Agamben," in *Giorgio Agamben: Sovereignty and Life*, eds. Matthew Calarco and Steven DeCaroli (Stanford, CA: Stanford University Press, 2007), 235.
34 Arne De Boever, *Plastic Sovereignties: Agamben and the Politics of Aesthetics* (Edinburgh: Edinburgh University Press, 2016), 23.
35 Ibid., 376.
36 Emily Apter, *Unexceptional Politics: On Obstruction, Impasse, and the Impolitic* (New York: Verso, 2018), 10.
37 Marie-Helene Huet, *The Culture of Disaster* (Chicago: University of Chicago Press, 2012), 8.
38 Janet Roitman, *Anti-Crisis* (Durham, NC: Duke University Press, 2014), 11.
39 Huet, *The Culture of Disaster*, 2.
40 Ibid., 39.
41 Roitman, *Anti-Crisis*, 90.
42 Bonnie Honig, *Emergency Politics: Paradox, Law, Democracy* (Princeton, NJ: Princeton University Press, 2009), xv.
43 Ibid., 80.
44 Elaine Scarry, *Thinking in an Emergency* (New York: Norton, 2011), 12–13.
45 Ibid., 106.
46 It must be pointed out there are other interpretations of the state of exception or emergency in Benjamin, Schmitt, and Agamben that develop their theories in different directions. See Didier Fassin and Mariella Pandolfi, eds., *Contemporary States of Emergency: The Politics of Military and Humanitarian Interventions* (New York: Zone Books, 2010); the special issue of *Philosophy Today* 59, no. 4 (Fall 2015), edited by Santiago Zabala, with contributions from Adrian Parr, Noreen Khawaja, Dorthe Jørgensen, Arne De Boever, Fredric Neyrat, Bonnie Honig, Diego Rosselo, Silvia Mazzini, Richard Polt, and Gianni Vattimo; the Special Issue of *ephemera: Theory and Politics in Collaboration*, "Whither Emergence?" *ephemera* 17, no. 4

(November 2017), edited by Ekaterina Chertkovskaya, Christian Garmann Johnsen, and Konstantin Stoborod, with contributions from Neera Singh, Nicolas Bencherki, and Beata Sirowi, among others; and Ryan Alford, *Permanent State of Emergency: Unchecked Executive Power and the Demise of the Rule of Law* (Montreal: McGill-Queen's University Press, 2017).

47 Martin Heidegger, "The Age of the World Picture," in *Off the Beaten Track*, eds. and trans., Julian Young and Kenneth Haynes (Cambridge: Cambridge University Press, 2002), 49.
48 Martin Heidegger, *The Event (1936–1938)*, trans. Richard Rojcewicz (Bloomington: Indiana University Press, 2013), 141.
49 Martin Heidegger, "Only a God Can Save Us: *Der Spiegel*'s Interview" (1976), in *Martin Heidegger: Philosophical and Political Writings*, eds. Manfred Stassen (New York: Continuum, 2003), 37.
50 Gregory Fried, *Heidegger's Polemos: From Being to Politics* (New Haven, CT: Yale University Press, 2000), 153–4.
51 Martin Heidegger, *Contributions to Philosophy (Of the Event)* (1989), trans. Richard Rojcewicz and Daniela Vallega-Neu (Bloomington: Indiana University Press, 2012), 89. I have changed "plight" for "emergency" in this passage.
52 Ibid., 99.
53 Martin Heidegger, "On the Question Concerning the Determination of the Matter for Thinking," trans. Richard Capobianco and Marie Göbel, in *Epoché* 14, no. 2 (Spring 2010): 218.
54 Heidegger, *Ponderings II–VI: Black Notebooks, 1931–1938* (Bloomington: Indiana University Press, 2016), 219. Rojcewicz translated *not* as "plight" while I prefer "emergency."
55 Heidegger, *Contributions to Philosophy (Of the Event)*, 22.
56 Paul Lewis et al., "Revealed: One in Four Europeans Vote Populist," *Guardian*, 20 November 2018, https://www.theguardian.com/world/ng-interactive/2018/nov/20/revealed-one-in-four-europeans-vote-populist.
57 Roger Cohen, "It's Time to Depopularize 'Populism,'" *New York Times*, 13 July 2018, https://www.nytimes.com/2018/07/13/opinion/populism-language-meaning.html.
58 Chantal Mouffe, *For a Left Populism* (New York: Verso, 2018), 85.
59 Ibid., 4.

60 Ernesto Laclau, *Post-Marxism, Populism, and Critique*, ed. D. Howarth (New York: Routledge, 2015), 266.
61 Richard Rorty, *Achieving Our Country: Leftist Thought in Twentieth-Century America* (Cambridge, MA: Harvard University Press, 1998), 90.
62 Nancy Fraser, "Against Progressive Neoliberalism: A New Progressive Populism," *Dissent*, 28 January 2017, https://www.dissentmagazine.org/online_articles/nancy-fraser-against-progressive-neoliberalism-progressive-populism. See also Fraser, "The End of Progressive Neoliberalism," *Dissent*, 2 January 2017, https://www.dissentmagazine.org/online_articles/progressive-neoliberalism-reactionary-populism-nancy-fraser.
63 Adrian Parr, *Birth of a New Earth: The Radical Politics of Environmentalism* (New York: Columbia University Press, 2018), 59.
64 Ibid., 62.
65 Stuart Primm, Maria Alice S. Alves, Eric Chivian, and Aaron Bernstein, "What Is Biodiversity?" in *Sustaining Life: How Human Health Depends on Biodiversity*, eds. Aaron Bernstein and Eric Chivian (New York: Oxford University Press, 2008), 26.
66 Carrington, Damian, "What Is Biodiversity and Why Does It Matter to Us?" *Guardian*, 12 March 2018, https://www.theguardian.com/news/2018/mar/12/what-is-biodiversity-and-why-does-it-matter-to-us.
67 Cristiana Paşca Palmer, quoted in Jonathan Watts's "Stop Biodiversity Loss or We Could Face Our Own Extinction, Warns UN," *Guardian*, 13 November 2018, https://www.theguardian.com/environment/2018/nov/03/stop-biodiversity-loss-or-we-could-face-our-own-extinction-warns-un.
68 Marco Lambertini, "A New Global Deal for Nature and People Urgently Needed," in WWF *Living Planet Report 2018: Aiming Higher*, eds. Monique Grooten and Rosamunde Almond (WWF, Gland, Switzerland. 2018), 4–5.
69 Matthias Aengenheyster1, Qing Yi Feng, Frederick van der Ploeg, and Henk A. Dijkstra, "The Point of No Return for Climate Action: Effects of Climate Uncertainty and Risk Tolerance," *Earth System Dynamics* 9 (August 2018): 1085.
70 Jennifer Morgan and Sharan Burrow, "Tackling the Twin Challenges of Climate Change and Inequality," *Al-Jazeera*, 21 January 2018,

https://www.aljazeera.com/indepth/opinion/tackling-twin-challenges-climate-change-inequality-190117124357686.html.
71 Geoffroy de Lagasnerie, *The Art of Revolt: Snowden, Assange, Manning* (Stanford, CA: Stanford University Press, 2017), 20–2.
72 Slavoj Žižek, *Trouble in Paradise: From the End of History to the End of Capitalism* (London: Penguin, 2014), 59.
73 Christopher Wylie, quoted in Olivia Solon, "Cambridge Analytica Whistleblower Says Bannon Wanted to Suppress Voters," *Guardian*, 16 May 2018, https://www.theguardian.com/uk-news/2018/may/16/steve-bannon-cambridge-analytica-whistleblower-suppress-voters-testimony.
74 On Brexit's relation to Cambridge Analytica, see Carole Cadwalladr, Emma Graham-Harrison, and Mark Townsend, "Revealed: Brexit Insider Claims Vote Leave Team May Have Breached Spending Limits," *Guardian*, 24 March 2018, https://www.theguardian.com/politics/2018/mar/24/brexit-whistleblower-cambridge-analytica-beleave-vote-leave-shahmir-sanni.
75 Christopher Wylie, quoted in Carole Cadwalladr, "Cambridge Analytica Has Gone. But What Has It Left in Its Wake?" *Guardian*, 6 May 2018, https://www.theguardian.com/uk-news/2018/may/06/cambridge-analytica-gone-what-has-it-left-in-its-wake.
76 Kevin Roose, "Facebook Emails Show Its Real Mission: Making Money and Crushing Competition," *New York Times*, 5 December 2018, https://www.nytimes.com/2018/12/05/technology/facebook-emails-privacy-data.html.

AFTERWORD

1 Gerald L. Bruns, *Hermeneutics: Ancient and Modern* (New Haven, CT: Yale University Press, 1992), 140.
2 Slavoj Žižek, *Like a Thief in Broad Daylight: Power in the Era of Post-Humanity* (London: Penguin, 2018), 26. On freedom as a "a signifier of disorientation," see Frank Ruda, *Abolishing Freedom. A Plea for a Contemporary Use of Fatalism* (Lincoln: University of Nebraska Press, 2016).

3 Robert Nichols, *The World of Freedom: Heidegger, Foucault, and the Politics of Historical Ontology* (Stanford, CA: Stanford University Press, 2014), 2.
4 Heidegger, *The Essence of Human Freedom*, 93.
5 Jean-Luc Nancy, *The Experience of Freedom*, trans. Bridget McDonald (Stanford, CA: Stanford University Press, 1993), 12.
6 Judith Butler, *Notes Toward a Performative Theory of Assembly* (Cambridge, MA: Harvard University Press, 2015), 60–1.

Index

absence of emergency (*Notlosigkeit*), 5, 9, 12, 69, 114–16, 135, 138–9, 155, 158

Achieving Our Country: Leftist Thought in Twentieth-Century America (Rorty), 143

Adorno, Theodore, 70

Agamben, Giorgio, 32, 113–17, 119, 122–7, 129–32, 134, 138, 146, 178n8

alteration, 65, 67–8, 97–8, 109, 116, 156; Augustine and, 105, 108, 109; Luther and, 102, 104, 109

alternative facts, 4, 9–10, 156; age of alternative facts, 3–4, 9–10, 12, 66, 159

American Philosophical Association, 80, 173n46

analytic philosophy, 43, 48, 66, 68, 74–9, 81

anarchy, 66, 68, 81–2, 121; Augustine's anarchic vein, 105, 109; Critchley, 66, 68, 82, 98; existence and, 11; Freud's anarchic vein, 87, 89; hermeneutics and, 12, 49, 62, 64–9, 156, 158; Luther's anarchic vein, 98; Nietzsche's anarchic vein, 82, 91, 95–6; Rorty's anarchic vein, 76; Schürmann, 64, 66, 68, 98, 171n18; Vattimo's anarchic vein, 74

Apel, Karl-Otto, 52–3, 62

Apter, Emily, 114, 126–8, 131

Aristotle, 21, 32, 63

Assange, Julian, 150–2, 154

Augustine, 63, 68, 97–101, 104–9

Bannon, Steve, 152, 154

Bauman, Zygmunt, 4

Being: at large, 54, 57, 156, 158, 159; Dasein as relation to, 18–19, 21, 23–7, 33, 36–7, 40, 48, 52–4, 57, 137; destiny of, 31; disclosure of, 31–2, 52–8; dissolution of, 42; as event, 30–2, 38, 40, 53, 71–4; genitive of, 24; grammatical categories of, 22; guardianship of, 24; intrinsic understanding of, 15, 49;

originary, 29–30; reason and, 18, 21, 27, 30, 56; thought of, 39, 135; tidings of, 23; understanding and, 31; working out, 27, 55. *See also* destruction of Being; generation of Being; meaning of Being; oblivion of Being; ontological difference; question of Being; understanding of Being; worn-out Being

Being and Time (Heidegger), 21, 35–8, 41, 49–50, 52–4

Benjamin, Walter, 67, 113–20, 122–3, 126, 178n8

Beyond Good and Evil (Nietzsche), 90

Bible, 67, 84, 97–8, 100–9; interpretation of, 97–8

biodiversity, 114, 139, 147, 149–50; ecosystem and, 14

Birth of Tragedy from the Spirit of Music, The (Nietzsche), 91

Black Notebooks (Heidegger), 16, 162n1

Blair, Tony, 141–2

Blondel, Eric, 91

Bowler, Michael, 33

Bruns, Gerald L., 64, 106, 156

Bush, George W., 71, 113, 123, 126

Butler, Judith, 157

Cabestan, Philippe, 85

Cadwalladr, Carole, 153

Cambridge Analytica, 151–4. *See also* whistleblowers

camp, detention and concentration, 124–5

capitalism, 69, 120, 130–1, 144

Caputo, John D., 63, 68

Charcot, Jean-Martin, 83

Clavis scripturae sacrae (Flacius), 63

climate change, 5, 70, 114, 138, 146–50; panel on, 149–50

Clinton, Hillary, 10, 145, 152

Cohen, Roger, 140

Confessions (Augustine), 105

conversation, 12, 19, 26–7, 33–5, 42, 44–8, 57, 68, 72, 75, 97; difference from dialogue, 33–4, 44–7, 62, 68, 72

Conway, Kellyanne, 4, 9, 10

Corbyn, Jeremy, 139, 143, 145

Critchley, Simon, 8–9, 66, 68, 82, 98

culture, 5, 10, 70–1, 75, 77, 80, 84, 87, 91–2, 96, 128–30, 135, 152, 155

Dannhauer, Johann, 63

Dasein, 18–19, 23–7, 33, 36–7, 40, 48, 52–4, 57, 137

Das Newe Testament Deutzsch (Luther), 103–4

Davis Hanson, Victor, 11

De Boever, Arne, 114, 126–8

deconstruction, 7, 16, 22, 29, 31, 35, 55

de Lagasnerie, Geoffroy, 151

Derrida, Jacques, 7, 16, 20, 28–30, 32, 35, 56, 78

destruction of Being, 20, 33, 44

Dewey, John, 34

dialogue, 33–4, 47, 62, 72, 74, 107; conversation compared with, 44–6, 68; in Plato, 45–6

différance, 29–30
Dilthey, Wilhelm, 34, 65, 82, 88, 104

Ebeling, Gegard, 104
economic crisis of 2008, 150
Eden, Kathy, 64, 108
emancipation, 42, 71, 88, 129; in relation to freedom, 92
emergency, 3, 5, 12, 113–15; greatest emergency, 5, 69, 114–15, 140, 145, 148, 158; Heidegger and, 69, 115–16, 135–9. See also absence of emergency; Agamben, Giorgio; Apter, Emily; Benjamin, Walter; biodiversity; De Boever, Arne; Huet, Marie-Hélène; populism; revelations; Roitman, Janet; Scarry, Elaine; Schmitt, Carl
Emergency of Being, The (Polt), 115
Essere e dintorni (Being and its surroundings), 20
event, 30–2, 35, 40, 52–3, 57, 125, 128–30, 132, 134, 146; Being and, 38–9, 71–4
existence, 9, 15, 18, 21–2, 37, 49–50, 54, 57, 66–8, 72, 92, 95–6, 119, 122, 127, 135, 138, 151, 156–7

facts, 4–7, 10; Kellyanne Conway and, 9; factual feminism and, 6; freedom and, 159; interpretation and, 65, 82, 94–5; intellectuals and, 6–7; return to order and, 156; and postmodernity, 10–12.
See also alternative facts; fake news
fake news, 9–12
Farewell to Truth (Vattimo), 47
Farin, Ingo, 33
feminism, 6, 144
Ferraris, Maurizio, 10–11
Fish, Stanley, 11
Flacius, 63
Foucault, Michel, 67, 122, 173n49
framed democracy, 141; neoliberal capitalism and, 69
Fraser, Nancy, 144–5
freedom, 12, 57–8, 73–4, 88, 96, 98, 109, 126, 139, 156–9; Agamben and, 126; Augustine and, 109; and emergency, 155; framed democracy and, 69; generated by Facebook, 154; Heidegger and, 54, 137, 157; hermeneutics as, 67, 73–4; interpretation as, 66–7, 73, 81, 156; Luther and, 98; Nietzsche and, 96; Žižek and, 152
Freud, Sigmund, 49, 66–8, 81–9, 91, 96, 174n56
Fried, Gregory, 17, 25, 137

Gadamer, Hans-Georg, 7, 16, 26, 32, 34–5, 37, 44–7, 57, 61–5, 68–9, 74, 76–7, 80–2, 97–8, 106–7, 169n1
generation of Being, 56
Giddens, Timothy, 141–2
globalization, 68, 70, 72–4, 81, 141–2, 144–5, 147, 149
Gonzalez, Francisco, 65

Greisch, Jean, 65
Grondin, Jean, 20, 44, 46, 106, 169n1
Gross, Neil, 80, 171n21
Guignon, Charles, 25
Gullì, Bruno, 126

Habermas, Jürgen, 16, 18, 52, 61–2
Hamburger, Jacob, 6
Harman, Graham, 6
Heidegger, Martin, 15–16, 47, 81, 97, 104; on Being, 17–22, 24–6, 32–6; on emergency, 69, 115–16, 135–9; on freedom, 54, 137, 157; on hermeneutics, 27, 41, 43, 63, 67; on Nazism, 15–16, 162n1; relation to Husserl, 50–2; on truth, 37
hermeneutics, 7, 20, 24, 27–8, 31–6, 41–4, 46–51, 55–7, 61–8; Augustine's, 104–9; Freud's, 82–8; Luther's, 98–104; Nietzsche's, 88–97; Rorty's, 75–81; Vattimo's, 68–75
Hermeneutics: Facts and Interpretation in the Age of Information (Caputo), 68
history, 73, 75, 78, 92–4, 117, 129, 137, 158; end of, 155–6; hermeneutics, 62–8, 81–2, 97; history of Being, 16, 22, 25, 27, 31, 36, 40, 73; as metaphysics, 21–3; open to the future, 33, 57; of the oppressed, 117–19
Hoff Sommers, Christina, 6–7
Honig, Bonnie, 114, 126, 131–3, 146

Huet, Marie-Hélène, 114, 126, 128–30
Husserl, Edmund, 7, 49–51

identity politics, 6, 139
intellectual dark web, 6, 9, 12, 158. *See also* new realism
interpretation, 6, 9, 11, 12, 20–2, 27–8, 33, 35, 41–4, 48, 51–2, 61–8, 156; anarchic vein, 12, 49, 62, 64, 66–8; as active practice, 156. *See also* hermeneutics
Interpretation of Dreams, The (Freud), 86

Jasper, David, 101
Jones, Ernest, 89

Kaufmann, Walter, 90
Kisiel, Theodore, 49
Kofman, Sarah, 90
Kotsko, Adam, 124
Krell, David Farrell, 16
Kuhn, Thomas, 49, 76–7

Laclau, Ernesto, 142
Lakoff, George, 10
Lambertini, Marco, 149
Latour, Bruno, 10
Löwy, Michael, 119
Luther, Martin, 36, 49, 66–8, 97–104, 109

Malabou, Catherine, 16, 126–7
Malpas, Jeff, 33, 63
Mann, Thomas, 89
Manning, Chelsea, 150–1, 154

Massing, Michael, 102
meaning of Being, 16, 21, 27–8
Meillassoux, Quentin, 8
Mélenchon, Jean-Luc, 139, 145
metaphysics, 12, 16–17, 19–44, 46–8, 50, 55–6, 58, 69, 70, 76, 90–1, 101
micropolitics, 127–8
Minelli, Filippo, 3, 159
modernity, 4, 93, 125
Mouffe, Chantal, 140, 142
Mr Robot, 3–4, 11, 159, 161n1; Elliot Alderson, 3, 12

naïve, 9–10
Nancy, Jean-Luc, 32, 57, 157
neoliberalism, 69, 130, 141; progressive, 144–5
new realism, 7–9, 11, 70–1, 73, 114; return to, 6, 9, 156; speculative realism, 7; object-oriented-ontology, 7
Nietzsche, Fredrich, 34, 36, 39, 62, 65, 68–9, 71, 73, 76, 81–2, 89–96, 169n1, 173n49

oblivion of Being, 15, 22, 55
On Christian Doctrine (Augustine), 104
On the Concept of History (Benjamin), 117
ontological difference, 21, 29–30, 32, 37–8, 41, 43

Pareyson, Luigi, 44, 48, 67
Parr, Adrian, 146–7
Paşca Palmer, Cristiana, 147

Peri hermeneias (De interpretatione), 63
phenomenology, 7, 48–51, 55
Pippin, Robert B., 90–1
planetary boundaries, 147
Plato, 17, 31–2, 38, 45–6, 65, 76, 107
Pöggeler, Otto, 37, 42, 53
Political Theology (Schmitt), 115–17, 178n8
Polt, Richard, 25, 115
Popper, Karl, 4
populism, 139–42; absence of, 139; difference between rightist and leftist, 139, 143, 145. *See also* Trump, Donald
postmodernism, 6, 10–11
power, 4, 11, 17, 26–7, 48–9, 54, 67, 69, 71–3, 77, 82, 91, 93–6, 113, 119–27, 129–30, 132–4, 136, 138–9, 142–3, 145–6, 149, 151
psychoanalysis, 82–5, 87–9, 96

question of Being, 17, 23–4, 36–9

remains, 12, 19, 22–4, 27–30, 32–5, 38–41, 43, 48, 56–8, 158
resentment, 9, 99, 140, 144–5
resistance, 12, 35, 48–9, 54–7, 67–8, 71, 73–4, 76, 81, 97, 124, 131, 133, 151
return to order, 4, 7–9, 12, 70–2, 155
revelations, 114, 150–4
Ricoeur, Paul, 44, 57, 81–2, 88, 173n49

Rockström, Johan, 147
Roitman, Janet, 114, 126, 128, 130–1
Roper, Lyndal, 98
Rorty, Richard, 5, 34–5, 48, 66, 67, 143–5; on analytic philosophy, 68, 74–81; on hermeneutics, 41–4, 47, 68, 75–8
Roudinesco, Élisabeth, 82, 174n56

Sallis, John, 53
Sanders, Bernie, 139, 143, 145
Scarry, Elaine, 114, 126, 131, 133–4, 146
Schleiermacher, Fredrich, 34, 65, 88, 104
Schmidt, Dennis J., 103
Schmitt, Carl, 113–17, 119–24, 126–7, 178n8
Schrift, Alan, 95
Schürmann, Reiner, 16, 35, 57, 64, 66, 68, 82, 98, 171n18
Schwarze Hefte (*Black Notebooks*) (Heidegger), 16, 162n1
science, 7, 10, 16–17, 48–9, 64, 69, 71–2, 77–9, 82–4, 87–90, 92, 129
Searle, John, 7, 33, 71–2
Snowden, Edward, 150–2, 154
society, 4–7, 88–9, 118, 120, 125, 132, 141, 155–6, 159
sovereign, 114–17, 119–28, 130–3, 135, 138, 141; and state of exception, 113–15, 119–21, 123–35, 138
Storr, Anthony, 84

Strong, Tracey B., 115

Thesis on the Philosophy of History (Benjamin), 117
transgression, 12, 64, 67–8, 82, 88, 96–7
translation, 66, 96–8, 102–4, 106–7, 109, 115–16, 135
Trump, Donald, 4–5, 10, 113–14, 125, 140, 143–5, 151–3
truth, 4–10, 12, 17, 19, 21, 37–8, 40, 44–6, 48–50, 135, 156; as correspondence, 37, 51–7; as disclosedness, 37, 52–5; freedom, 54, 152; Gadamer, 44, 64, 69; Heidegger and, 37, 50–3, 55–6; Nietzsche, 94–5; Rorty, 76–7, 81; Tugendhat, 50–2; Vattimo and, 31, 42–3, 71–3. *See also* dialogue
Truth and Method (Gadamer), 34, 63, 106
Tugendhat, Ernst, 34, 50–2

understanding of Being, 20–1, 28
Unexceptional Politics (Apter), 127

Valgenti, Robert, 69
Vattimo, Gianni, 5, 9, 16, 20, 28, 30–2, 34–6, 48, 53, 94; and weak thought, 42, 47; interpretation, 42–3, 68, 81; hermeneutics, 43–4, 62, 64, 66, 68–74, 78
Verwindung, 26–8, 30, 39, 55; difference from, *überwunden*, 26–8, 40, 50, 55

Warnke, Georgia, 33, 44, 48, 71
weak thought, 30–1, 35, 42, 44, 47, 56
Webb, David, 74
Weiss, Bari, 6
whistleblowers, 114, 139, 150–2
White, Hayden, 67
Woessner, Martin, 75
worn-out Being, 23–4, 26, 28, 39, 47
Wylie, Christopher, 151–4

Žižek, Slavoj, 8–9, 15, 152, 156
Zuckerberg, Mark, 10, 154